Practical legal English: legal terminolog

PRAKTIJKVAARDIGHEDEN

Practical legal English: legal terminology

Helen Gubby

Boom Juridische uitgevers
Den Haag
2006

Contents

5

Introduction

English has become the international language of trade and commerce. It is not surprising, therefore, that English has also become the international language of the legal transaction. This book is designed for non-native English speakers, for all those who have studied law, but not in English. The aim of the book is to offer students, and all those involved with the practice of the law, practical assistance in using English legal terminology.
Legal English and ordinary English are not identical languages. This is because legal English is a professional language, in the same way as the language of medical doctors is a professional one. It uses certain words and expressions that are either used differently in ordinary English or are not really used at all in everyday English. Even if someone's command of ordinary English is very good, this does not mean he knows how to use English legal terminology properly. Law firms, with an international clientele, correspond with their clients in English. Getting the legal terminology wrong could be a costly mistake.

How to use this book

The purpose of this book is to teach English legal terminology, not English law. Legal dictionaries are helpful, but they are organised alphabetically. In this book, the words are grouped into sets of words. The Vocabulary in each chapter gives you the kind of words you need to know in order to discuss that particular subject in English.
Yet English legal terminology can only be understood properly in the context of English law. The terminology comes from the common law and it cannot be treated as if it has nothing to do with English law. Even if you are using English legal terminology to describe, for example, Dutch law, you need to be aware of how that terminology is used in the English legal system. Otherwise, you might think you have chosen the right term to describe something in Dutch law, but actually you have not. The termi-

nology in context section gives a simple explanation of the legal terminology, while not getting the reader bogged down in the complexities of English law.

The legal subjects selected in the book are the type of core subjects most law students will study at some point in their education. Each chapter is devoted to one of these areas of law. It has a terminology in context section, a vocabulary, a case discussion and knowledge questions.

Terminology in context

The first item is the **terminology in context**. The words from the vocabulary are highlighted in this text so that you can see how the terminology fits into the structure of the law. It gives a brief outline of the relevant English law.

The English common law forms the basis for all other common law jurisdictions. However, the law in other common law countries, such as the USA and Australia, has developed in its own way over the years. This means that while there is still much shared terminology, there may also be variations in terminology. For example, a term used in the USA may not be used in England. As mentioned above, the outline given in the text is based on English law. It is beyond the scope of this book to give all the possible variations in all the other common law jurisdictions. Nonetheless, given the number of American legal textbooks in the libraries of higher educational institutions throughout the world, reference will be made to American legal terminology where differences in terminology could cause confusion.

The text particularly tries to take into account that many of the readers of this book will be students from civil law systems. Where English common law has a different approach to a legal issue from the more traditional civil law approach, a note will be given in the text. The standard example of a civil law system used in this book is that of the Netherlands.

Vocabulary

The second item in the chapter is a **vocabulary**. The vocabulary is ordered alphabetically, but it contains a set of words associated with that particular subject-matter. In this way, the relevant terminology is grouped together.

Case discussion

Following on from the vocabulary is the item **case discussion** (with the exception of the chapter on the legal system, which has general discussion questions). The case discussions serve as a practical exercise. For the self-study reader, the aim is that you should be able to see what the case is about and then answer the questions using the correct legal terminology. The terminology needed to do this is contained in the vocabulary and explained in the text. If the book is used as a course-work book, these cases form the basis for group discussion. Students, working together in small groups, are asked to analyse the case as a team and then present their findings in class. In this way, students become familiar with using the legal terminology.

Knowledge questions

The final item comprises the **knowledge questions**. This too is a practical exercise. It acts as a test for the reader, allowing you to check whether you have understood the terminology. If the book is used as a course-work book, these questions can be used as a basis for homework assignments.

Finally, it must be pointed out that the use of the word 'he' in the texts is not meant to be discriminatory to women. Its purpose here is to make the text more easily readable than where he/she, he/she or other well meant alternatives appear in a text.

1 Legal system terminology

At some point in time, you will be asked to explain your legal system in English. However, translating from one legal system to another legal system is far from easy. When, for example, a Dutch lawyer has to explain his legal system to an English lawyer, it is not simply a matter of replacing Dutch words with English words. The Dutch system is not the same as the English system. That means in order to use English legal terminology correctly and effectively, the Dutch lawyer must not only be familiar with his own legal system, but also have an understanding of the structure of the common law system. In this chapter, attention will be paid to the terminology of three elements associated with the legal system: the court structure, the legal profession and the operation of a common law system.

1.1 The civil law system and the common law system

In the West, the two most important types of legal systems are the common law system and the civil law system. The **common law** system originated in England. The common law developed as a system of case law; the judges in court were very important in establishing what was the law. The common law developed in the Middle Ages and was the law administered in the king's courts. This law gradually replaced local customary law. It was called the common law because it was common to all England and Wales and did not vary from area to area.

Over the course of time, the doctrine of **binding precedent** developed. This meant that judges deciding new cases should follow the decisions made by judges in the past, if these new cases were similar to those that had gone before. When the English set about establishing colonies, this common law system was often implemented in the colonies. Although there is no longer a British empire, the common law system has remained in force in various former colonies, for example, the USA, Canada and Australia.

The common law system should be distinguished from the **civil law** system. Civil law systems are **coded systems**, the laws being laid down in formal written codes. Unlike the common law system, the civil law system developed from Roman law. The code drafted under Napoleon in 1804, the 'Code Napoléon', must also be acknowledged as a source and example for many civil law systems in Europe and beyond.

The common law and the civil law systems are often treated as two entirely different approaches to the practice of law. However, these two systems are not as worlds apart as some lawyers maintain. Codes will always have to be interpreted and that will necessarily generate case law. And anyone who thinks a common law system derives its law only from the courts would be very wide of the mark. As can be seen below, **legislation** plays a vital role in all common law systems today.

1.2   The court structure

Trying to find a good English translation for the name of a court in a different legal system can sometimes be quite difficult. For this reason, the following sections describe the courts and their **competence** in the English and American court systems.

1.2.1   England

Although there are courts specialised in criminal cases or civil cases, most courts actually hear both. English courts are classed as either **superior** or **inferior** courts. The **jurisdiction** of the superior courts is not limited to a specific geographical area or to the value of the claim being brought. The jurisdiction of the inferior courts is limited in this way. The distinction between superior and inferior is also important, as the decision of a superior court is **binding**; in other words, the lower courts must follow the decisions of the higher courts. This is called the doctrine of **binding precedent** (see next page).

```
┌─────────────────────────────────────────────┐
│              House of Lords:                 │
│  superior court. It is the highest national  │
│  appeal court; its decisions are binding on  │
│            all other courts.                 │
└─────────────────────────────────────────────┘
                      ▼
┌─────────────────────────────────────────────┐
│              Court of Appeal:                │
│     superior court, but it is bound by the   │
│         decisions of the House of Lords.     │
└─────────────────────────────────────────────┘
                      ▼
┌─────────────────────────────────────────────┐
│               High Court:                    │
│   superior court. It is bound by the House   │
│     of Lords and the Court of Appeal.        │
└─────────────────────────────────────────────┘
            ▼                    ▼
┌───────────────────────┐  ┌──────────────────┐
│     Crown Court:      │  │  County Court:   │
│ superior court. The   │  │  inferior court. │
│ most serious criminal │  │ It hears mainly  │
│ offences are tried by │  │ civil law cases. │
│ a jury in the Crown   │  │                  │
│ Court. It is bound by │  │                  │
│ the decisions of the  │  │                  │
│ higher courts.        │  │                  │
└───────────────────────┘  └──────────────────┘
            ▼                    ▼
┌─────────────────────────────────────────────┐
│             Magistrates' Court:              │
│  inferior court. It hears low level civil    │
│         and criminal law cases.              │
└─────────────────────────────────────────────┘
```

Note 1: in addition to this mainstream structure, there are a number of other courts and tribunals. For example, the Restrictive Practices Court, the **Employment Tribunal** and the Employment Appeal Tribunal, which have specialised jurisdictions.

Note 2: the United Kingdom is a member of the European Union. Although not a national court, the court at the apex of the English court structure for all matters concerning the law of the European Union is the **European Court of Justice**. Its role is to ensure the legal enforcement of European Union obligations and the uniform interpretation of European law throughout the Member States of the European Union.

Note 3: there is no parallel separate system of administrative courts as in some countries, such matters being mainly dealt with by High Court judges.

1.2.2   USA

The distinction between the federal level and the state level means there are both federal courts and state courts in the USA. The jurisdiction of the **federal courts** is set out in the US Constitution. **State courts**, unlike the federal courts, have a far more general competence. They have the competence to hear most legal disputes.

There may be concurrent jurisdiction between federal and state courts. For example, if in a car theft, the car has been driven from one state to another, the case could be tried either in a federal court or in the state court of one of the states involved. Federal courts are typically used where the parties to a dispute are citizens of different states or are US citizens and non-US citizens. The overlapping of competence has given rise to so-called **forum shopping**, where parties select the court they believe to be most favourable to their claim.

Federal court structure

US Supreme Court:
it hears important questions concerning constitutional or federal law. There is no absolute right to be heard by the US Supreme Court; it hears only a limited number of cases that it is asked to decide.

US Courts of Appeal:
these are spread throughout the USA. An appeal court mainly hears appeals from the district courts located within its circuit.

District Courts:
these are the trial courts of the federal court system. There is at least one district court in each state. They have the jurisdiction to hear nearly all categories of federal cases, both criminal and civil. Cases may be heard either by a single judge or a judge and jury.

N Note: other federal courts include: **US Bankruptcy Courts, US Tax Court, US Claims Court, Court of International Trade.**

State court structure
Each state has its own court system. Some state court systems have many different courts, whereas others may only have three courts: a supreme court, a court of appeal and a district court. The names of courts also vary widely. State courts deal with the vast majority of all court cases in the USA.

Translation note
It is common to find the names of the US federal court system used for translation purposes. In general, the highest court in a country is usually translated by the term **Supreme Court**, the appellate court level by **Court of Appeal** and the trial initialisation level by **District Court**. However, court systems vary from country to country and sometimes there is simply no equivalent court in the Anglo/American system that can be used for translation purposes.

That means that the best translation may be a simple description of the function of the court, such as the 'Constitutional Court of Spain'. In other cases, the best approach may be to use general terms to describe the position of the court in the court hierarchy. In this way, someone unfamiliar with that court system will be able to gather what kind of status of court is being referred to.

- Important courts can be referred to by the terms: high court/ superior court/senior court/court of higher jurisdiction.

- Courts of lesser status can be referred to by the terms: lower court/inferior court/court of lower jurisdiction. The term **court of first instance** can be used to describe a court in which proceedings are started.

It is recommended that the English translation of the name of the court should always be accompanied by the actual name of the court in the original language (put in brackets after the English translation). For example, the Supreme Court of the Netherlands (Hoge Raad).

1.2.3 Alternatives to the courts

The idea behind alternative dispute resolution (**ADR**) was that it would be less formal, quicker than the mainstream courts and less expensive. There are three types of ADR: **mediation, conciliation** and **arbitration**.

1.3 The legal profession

Lawyers often find that translating their business cards into English is not as easy as they had expected. The way the legal profession is arranged in one country may be quite different from the way it is arranged in another country. For example, in the Netherlands there are two main strands in the legal profession: notaries (notarissen) and advocates (advocaten). As the English legal profession is also split into two main strands, solicitors and barristers, it would seem the translation is ready-made. Unfortunately, that is not the case as the competence of solicitors and barristers is divided in a different way from that of the Dutch notaries and advocates.

A Dutch notary does indeed do the type of work that would be typical of some of the work of an English solicitor, but a Dutch notary would not prepare work for litigation, whereas an English solicitor would, and an English solicitor may also act as an advocate in the lower courts. On the other hand, a Dutch advocate may have the type of practice which resembles that of an English solicitor far more than it does that of an English barrister. In an international context, Dutch law firms tend to use anglicised versions of their professional functions: notaries and advocates.

> **N** Note: the term 'notary' does not denote a separate strand of the legal profession in the USA or England. A 'notary public' has authority to witness and draw up certain documents, and so make them official. In England this is usually done by a solicitor. In the USA this can be done by an attorney, but it can also be done by a private individual who has applied to act as a notary, for example, a real estate agent or clerks in a shop. Those Dutch law firms that are aware of this tend to use the expression 'civil law notaries'. This has the advantage of making their common law colleagues

take note that some sort of unfamiliar function is involved here, but the term is not one that will be self-evident to them. You will need to explain it.

1.3.1 England

In the English legal system, a practicing lawyer must have one of two professional qualifications: he must either have been admitted to practice as a **solicitor** or have been called to the bar as a **barrister**. An English lawyer may not act both as a solicitor and as a barrister.

Solicitor

A solicitor may be described as a general legal adviser. Solicitors' offices are usually partnerships and senior solicitors act as partners in the firm. Their usual areas of work are **conveyancing** (law and procedure with respect to the purchase and sale of property), **probate** (procedure to verify a document, often a will, and the winding up and distribution of a deceased person's estate), the negotiation and **drafting** of company and commercial contracts and the preparation of **litigation** (court cases), although in the larger firms of solicitors some solicitors have specialised. They may work as advocates but, without an advocacy certificate, they have only a limited right of audience in the courts.

Barrister

Unlike solicitors, barristers are self-employed, but group together for administrative convenience in **chambers** where they share the accommodation, secretariat and the services of the clerk. It is incorrect therefore to refer to a firm of barristers. Possibly the most important person in chambers is the **clerk**. He acts as a business manager and is now often referred to as the **practice manager**: he attracts the work, arranges the **briefs** (written instructions from a solicitor to a barrister giving him a case) for individual barristers and negotiates the fee with the solicitors, as a barrister's fee is not paid directly by his client but through the solicitor.

The work of many barristers is that of an advocate, arguing a client's case in court. Barristers have a **right of audience** in all courts. When representing a party in court, the barrister is referred to as **counsel** (for the client or in criminal cases for the defence or prosecution). Barristers are often specialists in certain legal domains.

> [N] Note: the difference between solicitors and barristers is often compared to that between the family doctor and the hospital specialist. For most legal matters, members of the public will visit a solicitor. The solicitor will call in the aid of a barrister if he needs expert advice and/or the client's case will become a court case and the expertise of a barrister is required.

1.3.2 USA

The USA broke with the tradition of distinguishing between solicitors and barristers. A practicing lawyer in the USA is an **attorney**. In the USA, an attorney performs either the functions of a solicitor or a barrister or both functions. The terms 'lawyer' and 'attorney' may be used interchangeably.

An attorney may only practice law in the state for which he has been admitted to the bar. For example, an attorney admitted to the Florida State Bar has no right to act as an attorney in California. Separate admission to practice in the federal courts must also be obtained. Lawyers who work for companies in their legal departments or for a government agency must also be members of the bar: they are referred to as in-house counsel or staff attorneys.

> [N] Note: in the USA, the word 'esquire' (esq) used after the name denotes that that person has been admitted to practice law. However, the word esquire does not have that meaning in England, where it is sometimes used as an alternative to putting Mr. before the name of a man.

1.3.3 Judges in the common law system

The role of the judge in the common law system is somewhat different from that in many civil law systems. The judge is neither adviser nor investigator. In general, the judge must rely upon the advocates to present legal and factual argument, although if a vital precedent has been ignored, he can ask for counsel's arguments on it. The judge acts as an impartial referee in an **adversarial** judicial process (see Vocabulary, Chapter 2). He must base his decision-making on the evidence presented to the court by legal counsel, apply the existing rules of law to those facts, and then give his judgment.

In England, most senior judges are recruited from experienced practicing barristers, although opportunities for solicitors to become judges have increased more recently. In the USA, federal judges are appointed by the President and the Senate for life. As for state judges, the method of appointment depends on the state. Judges may be chosen from outstanding members of the bar by the governor, or by the mayor for lower courts, or elected by the public, or a combination of both methods. This system of appointment is quite different from some civil law jurisdictions, for example the Netherlands, where law graduates can train specifically to become a judge and where a judge is a civil servant.

> `N` Note 1: at the bottom of the judicial hierarchy in England are the magistrates. Many of these justices, who sit in the **magistrates'** courts, are lay people, in other words they are not qualified lawyers. They are responsible and respected people in their community, sitting on average one day per fortnight. Magistrates are not paid, but only receive expenses. They are advised by magistrates' clerks, who are usually law graduates, or have a special clerk's diploma. In the USA, there is no system of lay justices similar to the system of lay magistrates in England.

> `N` Note 2: mention should be made of the Law Officers. In the English system, one of the most important Law Officers is the **Attorney-General**. He is a legal adviser to the Crown. The Attorney-General has political duties which include advising government departments. Similarly, in the USA there is also an Attorney-General. He is the head of legal affairs in a state or in the federal government. If he is in the federal government, he is in charge of the Department of Justice. The USA also has a district attorney. This is an officer of a governmental body, such as a state, county or municipality, with the duty to prosecute all those charged with crimes. District attorneys working for the federal government are called US attorneys.

1.4 The jury

A mistake that is often made by law students from civil law systems without a jury is to equate a jury system with a common law system. Juries are, however, not confined to common law jurisdictions. For example, in Spain and Belgium juries hear certain types of cases. What can be said, however, is that both in England and the USA court room proceedings are geared up to the presence of a jury, whether one is actually in sitting or not.

In England, the appearance of a jury in civil cases is now rare. There is no right to jury trial for most civil cases, although certain lawsuits, such as **defamation** (see Vocabulary, Chapter 3), can still be heard by a jury. In criminal cases, only very serious criminal offences are heard by a jury. A jury consists of twelve **jurors** who are laymen and who are supposed to represent a cross-section of the community. In civil cases, the jury decides upon liability and sometimes assesses the **damages** (financial compensation) under the guidance of the judge. In criminal cases, the jurors listen to the facts of the case and, after the judge's summing up of the prosecution and defence cases, they have to reach a verdict: guilty or not guilty. The jury has no say in questions dealing with law or legal procedure or on sentencing in criminal cases.

In the USA, the right to jury trial is guaranteed by the US Constitution. Many civil trials are before juries, but if both parties agree to do away with the jury, as this is cheaper and quicker, the case will be decided by the judge. With respect to criminal cases, the Sixth Amendment of the Constitution guarantees a defendant the right to trial by jury. However, as in England, juries do not hear cases for minor crimes. Some states, for example Washington, have a **grand jury** of up to twenty-three jurors to see if there is a case to answer before going to trial. A **petit jury** is the ordinary trial jury, usually composed of twelve jurors (but some state court juries may consist of six jurors).

In both England and the USA there are proceedings for the selection of jurors, although this procedure is far more extensive in the USA than in England. In the USA, the French term **voir dire** usually refers to the examination by the court or by the attorneys of prospective jurors. In England it is more commonly referred to as **jury vetting**. Jurors can be **challenged** either by the defence or by the prosecution. They can be challenged 'for cause' (for a reason) or 'without cause' (reason not stated).

1.5   Operation of a common law system

A common law system is based on three major sources of law:
- **common law** (or **case law**)
- **equity** and
- **legislation**.

At one time, common law courts and equity courts were separate. The law administered in the common law courts was based on principles derived from case law. Equity courts administered their own law, based on principles of fairness. Now all law courts apply both common law and the principles of equity in their courts. As this distinction between common law and equity is a characteristic of the common law system, and one unfamiliar to those schooled in the civil law, attention is paid below to the development of equity and its terminology. The third major source of law is legislation. Legislation is formal, written law, as opposed to law that has been developed by the judges in court. Today, legislation has become a major part of the law of any common law jurisdiction.

1.5.1   Legislation

Even though the English and American legal systems are common law systems, **legislation** plays an important role in law making. **Statutes** are laws made by legislative bodies, such as the Parliament in England and the Congress in the USA. The most common form of statute is the **Act**, which is called a **bill** before it has been passed. When a statute is drawn up, the old common law usually forms the basis for the statute, but the legislature takes the opportunity to modify and update the old law. It is also increasingly common for whole areas of law to be put into statute form, for example tax law. Statutes often adopt the old common law terminology, which means that they are very difficult to understand for those with no knowledge of the common law.

The English system

In England the legislative body is the Parliament, composed of the House of Commons and the House of Lords, the laws being approved by the Crown. The **doctrine of parliamentary sovereignty** means that supreme power is vested in Parliament. Until recently, this doctrine stated that only Parliament could make or **revoke** any law by statute, although it could not bind future parliaments. Whatever law Parliament has passed in the form of an Act must be put into effect by the courts and the courts cannot overrule legislation once passed.

However, this doctrine has had to undergo a certain modification because of England's membership of the European Union (EU). The supremacy of EU law above that of national law means that the national courts of Member States are required to **override** national legislation where it conflicts with EU law. This has extended the rights of English courts with respect to **judicial review**, as the court may, for example, hold that certain provisions of an **Act of Parliament** are inoperative because they are in breach of EU obligations.

N Note 1: in English national legislation and in the legislation of some of the states of the USA, reference is made to 'sections' of a statute rather than to 'articles'. However, in American federal legislation and in the treaties and directives of the European Union reference is made to 'articles' rather than to sections.

N Note 2: there is also delegated legislation, meaning that the parliament gives subordinate authorities the power to make laws. The most important form of delegated legislation is the **statutory instrument**, i.e. ministers are given the power to make laws for specified purposes.

The system in the USA

In the USA, legislation takes place at two levels: the federal and the state. Just as EU law is superior to the national legislation of the Member States, federal legislation is superior to state legislation in its areas of competence. It is said to **pre-empt** state legislation where there is a conflict. Any state legislation which conflicts with the federal laws is void. It should also be noted that the

US Supreme Court has the power to throw out any legislation not in keeping with the US Constitution.

The federal legislative body is the **Congress**, consisting of the House of Representatives and the Senate. The federal legislature has at its head the president, with the duty to make sure that the laws are carried out properly and the power to make treaties and veto laws.

States, headed by a governor, have their own legislatures (consisting of two houses, except in Nebraska). States have jurisdiction over all matters not reserved to the federal competence. In the USA, each state has its own set of statutes and most jurisdictions have now codified a substantial part of their laws. Uniform laws are also important. As each state has its own law, the idea behind the development of uniform laws was to cut down the differences in law between the various states of America. The most successful uniform law is the Uniform Commercial Code (UCC).

1.5.2 Equity

During the medieval period, the common law became rather rigid and inflexible. If a writ could not be issued, a person had no **legal remedy**. For example, someone who had bought the right to use land but did not own that land, could not obtain a writ to have his case heard in court. This was because a court of common law only recognised a legal title to land; it would only enforce the rights of the 'owner' of the land. Those who had no remedy at common law turned to the king's chancellor for help. Under the chancellor, a court of equity developed, where principles of fairness referred to as **principles of equity** were applied. Equity and common law remained administered in separate courts for centuries. Today, all courts can apply rules from the common law and principles of equity. The terminology that was developed in the courts of equity forms a part of English legal terminology.

The courts of equity recognised that the same piece of property could represent two interests: a legal interest and an equitable interest. The person with the legal interest has a **legal title** to the property which was the one recognised at common law. The other person has an equitable interest and an **equitable title** was recognised by the courts of equity, but not by the common law courts. An example of this splitting of interests is where a trust has been set up.

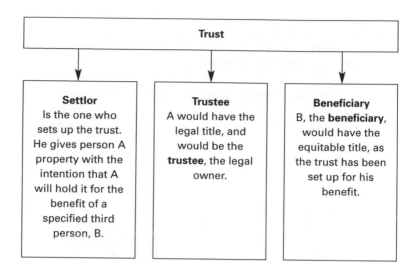

Trust		
Settlor Is the one who sets up the trust. He gives person A property with the intention that A will hold it for the benefit of a specified third person, B.	**Trustee** A would have the legal title, and would be the **trustee**, the legal owner.	**Beneficiary** B, the **beneficiary**, would have the equitable title, as the trust has been set up for his benefit.

An equitable title is well protected by the law. However, the legal title usually prevails where there is a conflict between legal and equitable interests if the legal title is sold to a purchaser and bought in good faith. In common law jurisdictions, trusts are often set up for a variety of purposes: for individuals, charities, clubs, unit trust schemes and as security for a particular loan.

The equity court also developed legal remedies that were not available in common law courts. The main remedy at common law is damages. Equity offered remedies other than damages, such as the **injunction** and **specific performance** (these terms are dealt with in other chapters). The merger of common law and equity courts meant that equitable remedies became available in all courts. Nonetheless, they cannot be claimed as a right: equitable remedies have remained **discretionary**.

Note 1: the word 'equity' will be found used in a variety of ways, not just in the sense of a parallel system of law to the common law. For example, equity is also used to refer to the value of property minus any charges that are on it, equity capital is that part of a company's capital that is owned by shareholders and equities are shares.

N Note 2: trusts make use of splitting the same property into two interests, legal and equitable. Some jurisdictions do not allow this use of split interests, for example the Netherlands, although foreign trusts may be recognised.

N Note 3: US antitrust laws do not refer to trusts as outlined above. The term 'antitrust laws' refers in particular to two statutes that deal with agreements or cooperative attempts to undermine free competition in the marketplace.

1.5.3 The common law

Despite the increasing growth of legislation in common law jurisdictions, **case law** is still extremely important. Case law refers to the decisions made by judges, applying legal principles to the particular facts of the dispute before them. Common law lawyers must be familiar with past cases because the rules of law laid down in these cases remain the law unless they have been overruled. This means that decisions made in very old cases can still represent the law.

N Note: the English term **jurisprudence** does not mean case law. The section on 'Jurisprudence' in an English library will direct you to books on the study or philosophy of law. In the USA the term jurisprudence can be found used in the English sense as a science of law, but also in the sense of case law rather than statute law. This dual use of the term is now creeping into English texts due to the influence of American English and the European Court.

Binding precedent

When a judge comes to try a case he must always look back to see how previous judges have dealt with earlier cases with similar facts. These decisions set a **precedent** and a judge will be expected to make a decision consistent with the precedents set already. This doctrine is called the doctrine of **binding precedent**. It is also known by the Latin term **stare decisis**. Precedents set by the senior courts are always binding on all lower courts.

Must a precedent always be followed? The answer to that is no; not if a case can be **distinguished**. Cases can only be distinguished on their facts. The facts or a fact in the new case must, in some important way, be different from the facts or a fact of the previous case. The court regards as a material fact any important fact that makes the new case different from the previous one. The word **material** is used in legal English to indicate that something is important or vital, for example material facts, material evidence, material witness. The Americans often use the term **key** in this context.

Case reports
Obviously, in a system where case law is so important there must be a sophisticated system of law reports. In England and the USA, precedents are almost always contained in law reports, and these reports are now of a fairly standardised nature. Each case is given a reference. The form of this reference will depend upon whether the case is a criminal case or a civil case. The reference is followed by the year the case was heard and (an abbreviation of) the name of the series in which the case is reported. An example of a civil case reference is as follows:

Donoghue v Stevenson [1932] A.C. 562.

If it is a criminal case, the reference would be different as the prosecution is then brought in the name of the state (here 'R' stands for the Latin word regina or rex, i.e. the Queen or King), for example:

R v Beard [1920] A.C. 479.

When the judgment is published in a law report, it begins with a head-note, which is a summary of the case. In English reports, this head-note is followed by the individual judgment of the judge or judges in that case. By reporting each individual judgment, it is possible to see exactly what each judge thought. When judges agree with each other they are said to **concur**. When a judge disagrees with the majority decision, he is said to **dissent**.

Every case report has three major sections:

```
┌─────────────────────────────────────────────────────────────┐
│                    1 The material facts                     │
│        What are the relevant facts of this particular case? │
└─────────────────────────────────────────────────────────────┘
                              │
                              ▼
┌─────────────────────────────────────────────────────────────┐
│                    2 The ratio decidendi                    │
│  This sets out the grounds for the decision, the legal      │
│  reasoning that has been applied to the facts of the case.  │
│  In the USA, the ratio decidendi is more commonly           │
│  referred to as a holding.                                  │
└─────────────────────────────────────────────────────────────┘
                              │
                              ▼
┌─────────────────────────────────────────────────────────────┐
│                    3 The judgment                           │
│              This is based on sections 1 and 2.             │
│  The judge finds in favour of the claimant or defendant in  │
│  civil cases, or the state or the accused in criminal cases.│
└─────────────────────────────────────────────────────────────┘
```

For the parties, part 3 is vital. For the purpose of the doctrine of binding precedent, part 2 is vital. It is this part that forms the precedent of the case.

> **N** Note: sometimes a judge makes hypothetical remarks or his judgment is a dissenting judgment because he disagrees with the majority decision. Such comments or a dissenting judgment are called obiter dicta because they are not part of the ratio decidendi. Comments that are **obiter dicta** are not binding, but they are **persuasive**.

Appeal
A decision is **reversed** when a higher court on appeal comes to the opposite conclusion than that of the lower court. So now, for example, instead of finding for the claimant, it finds in favour of the defendant.
An appeal court can also **overrule** a principle that has been established in a previous case. This means that the precedent laid down in that earlier case is no longer binding. Reversing differs from overruling. A decision reversed on appeal directly affects the

parties involved in that case. Overruling goes only to the rule of law contained in a decision; it does not affect the parties who were involved in those cases.

N Note 1: in the USA, overruling also applies to a court's denial of any motion or point raised in court, for example, 'objection overruled'.

N Note 2: a system of **cassation** courts is not used for appeal cases in England and the USA (see Chapter 2).

LEGAL SYSTEM VOCABULARY

Act: a specific piece of legislation passed by a legislative body, such as Parliament or Congress. An **Act of Parliament** is divided into **parts**, **sections**, **sub-sections**, **paragraphs** and, at the end, the **schedules**.

ADR: these initials stand for **alternative dispute resolution**. This includes **mediation**, **conciliation** and **arbitration**.

Arbitration: a form of alternative dispute resolution where a third party, acting as an arbitrator, delivers an opinion that is binding on the parties.

Attorney-at-law: usually referred to simply as an attorney. An attorney is a legal professional in the USA with the right to practice law in the state for which he has been admitted to the bar.

Attorney-General: in England he is a legal adviser to the Crown. The Attorney-General has political duties which include advising government departments. In the USA there is also an Attorney-General. He is the head of legal affairs in a state or in the federal government.

Barrister: a legal professional in the English legal system with a right of audience before all courts. As well as acting as an advocate, a barrister may also be a specialist in a certain area of law.

Beneficiary: one who benefits from a **trust** and who has an **equitable interest** in the trust property.

Bill: an Act of Parliament is called a bill before it has been formally approved.

Binding: if a decision is binding, it must be followed. For example, an arbitrator's decision is binding on the parties involved.

Binding precedent: the precedent (see **precedent**) laid down in a prior case of a similar nature must be followed. The Latin term for the doctrine of binding precedent is **stare decisis**.

Brief: in the English system this refers to the written instructions sent by a solicitor to a barrister briefing him about a case.

Case law: refers to the decisions made by judges applying legal principles from **legislation** and the **precedents** from previous cases to the circumstances of the particular disputes before them.

Challenge: potential members of a jury can be challenged, either for a reason that is stated before the court or for no reason. This is a way of excluding potential jurors from a jury.

Chambers: accommodation for a group of barristers. Barristers in chambers are self-employed and group together only to share facilities and staff. It would therefore be wrong to refer to a firm of barristers.

Civil law: this term has two meanings. It can be used in the sense of the law concerned with private rights rather than public law. The term may also be used to describe a legal system. Unlike the common law system, a civil law system has its roots in Roman law and is a codified system.

Clerk: the English legal system knows various types of legal clerks, for example, a magistrate's clerk assists lay magistrates. The clerk in barristers' chambers, often now referred to as the **practice manager**, acts as a business manager for the barristers of that chamber.

Coded systems: systems where the codification of the law has taken place, i.e. the laws of the land have been compiled to form a systematic, formal legal code.

Common law: a system of law which originated in medieval England and was later applied in former British colonies, including the USA. Common law is based on case law rather than on codes.

Competence: a court has the competence to hear a case if it has **jurisdiction** over the person or property at issue in that case.

Conciliation: alternative form of dispute resolution where a third party, acting as a conciliator, offers the parties a non-binding opinion.

Concur: verb used to indicate that judges in a case agree with the majority conclusion. The reasons for reaching that conclusion may, however, vary.

Congress: the federal legislative body of the USA. It consists of two houses, the Senate and the House of Representatives.

Conveyancing: drawing up legal documents to transfer the ownership of property from seller to buyer; in general the law and procedure with respect to the purchase and sale of property.

Counsel: when representing a party in court, a barrister is referred to as counsel and an attorney as counsel or counsellor.

County Court: in the English system it hears civil cases in its local area of jurisdiction. The name County Court may also be found in the court systems of several states in the USA, where it has a limited jurisdiction in civil and criminal cases.

Court of Appeal: this is an appellate court to be found in many common law jurisdictions. It hears appeals from lower courts.

Court of first instance: this term can be used to describe a court in which proceedings begin.

Crown Court: this is a court in the English court system that hears primarily criminal cases.

Discretionary: where a remedy is not available as of right but depends upon the consideration of the court.

Dissent: where a judge disagrees with the majority opinion in a case. A **dissenting judgment** is classed as **obiter dicta**.

Distinguish: if a case is distinguished, a judge finds a precedent laid down in a previous case not binding on the case before him because the **material/key facts** in the present case differ from those of the previous case.

District courts: these are the trial courts of the American federal court system.

Doctrine of parliamentary sovereignty: all legislative power in England is vested in Parliament or is derived from the authority of Parliament. Parliament in this context means the House of Commons, the House of Lords and the Crown. Parliament has the right to make any laws it wishes to make, although in practice these laws must be in keeping with accepted customs and values and not contrary to European Union law.

Draft: when a legal document, such as a contract, is being drawn up, the preliminary version (or versions) of the document is referred to as a draft. The draft may be subject to amendments before it is accepted as the final version.

Employment Tribunal: tribunal in the English system with the jurisdiction to hear almost all individual employment law claims.

Equitable title: under the principles of law developed by the court of equity, one piece of property could be subject to two sorts of interest: a legal interest and an **equitable interest**. The legal owner of the property holds the **legal title**, which was protected by the common law. The one with the equitable interest holds an equitable title, which was protected by the chancellor in the court of equity. The person holding the equitable title is the one intended to benefit from the property, even though that person is not the legal owner. An equitable title is still protected in law against everyone except a purchaser of the property who had no knowledge of the equitable interest.

Equity: historically, equity developed as a separate system of law in England as the common law was too rigid. The court of equity developed its own principles of fairness and its own legal remedies. Now all courts may apply **principles of equity** alongside those of the common law.

European Court of Justice: is the highest court for all those countries that are members of the European Union. It has the competence to make decisions regarding European Union law.

Federal courts: the courts of the USA as distinguished from the courts of the individual states. Federal courts hear cases that involve disputes or issues governed by federal law or the US Constitution or disputes involving citizens from different states.

Forum shopping: where more than one court has the competence to hear a case and parties wish to select the forum which would be most favourable for their case.

High Court: a superior court in the English court system.

House of Lords: the House of Lords as a court should be distinguished from its function as the upper house of Parliament. Only those members of the upper house who are Law Lords may hear appeals. The court hears appeals for both civil and criminal cases where the matter is of public importance.

Inferior: an adjective used to describe a lower court. It does not mean that the quality of the court is poor. It simply means a court of lower jurisdiction.

Judicial review: this term is used in particular to describe the situation when judges review decisions made by public authorities that affect the rights of individuals.

Jurisdiction: the legal power to hear and decide a case. If the court does not have the jurisdiction to hear a case, its decision will be void.

Jurisprudence: the study or philosophy of law. In the USA it is also used in the sense of case law rather than statute law.

Juror: a member of a jury.

Jury: a cross-section of the public called upon to hear a case.

Jury vetting: procedure by which members of the public are selected in court for jury service in England. In the USA, the counsels for the defence/prosecution have far more opportunities to challenge potential members of the jury than in England. This procedure is commonly termed **voir dire** in the USA.

Legal remedy: means provided by the law to help one party because the other party has acted contrary to the rules of law.

Legislation: written laws passed by a legislative body, for example, the Parliament in England and the Congress in the USA.

Litigation: where a party, known as a litigant, brings an action (a lawsuit) to the court.

Magistrate: a judge in England and the USA. In the English court system, magistrates are often lay people.

Magistrates' Court: in the English court system this is an inferior court that hears both civil and criminal cases. However, it should be borne in mind that the magistrates' courts handle most of the cases brought to court.

Material: used generally to denote something of importance in a case, for example, material fact or a material witness. The word **key** may also be used in this context.

Mediation: alternative form of dispute resolution where a third party, acting as a mediator, helps the parties to a dispute to reach an agreement.

Obiter dicta: plural of obiter dictum, meaning passing or incidental remarks in a judicial opinion that do not form part of the **ratio decidendi**. Unlike the ratio decidendi, obiter dicta are not binding.

Override: see **pre-emption**.

Overrule: a court reaches the decision that a precedent laid down in a different case no longer has to be followed.

Persuasive: if the authority is persuasive rather than binding, the judge is not obliged to follow it, but it should be taken into account in reaching a judgment.

Precedent: a decision in a previous case which is recognised as being a source of legal authority for all future cases of a similar nature.

Pre-emption: where one system of law takes precedence over another. In the USA, federal legislation is superior to state legislation and will pre-empt state legislation where there is a conflict. In Europe, the law of the European Union is said to **override** that of the national law of the Member States on matters within its competence.

Probate: legal acceptance that a document, usually associated with the administration of estates, such as a will, is valid.

Ratio decidendi: the reason, or grounds, for the decision. This is the part of the judgment in which legal principles are applied to the facts of a particular case. It is this part of the judgment which forms the precedent. In the USA this may also be referred to as a **holding**.

Reverse: when a higher court, hearing a case on appeal from a lower court, reaches the opposite judgment to that of the lower court.

Revoke: to cancel or annul, for example to annul previous legislation.

Right of audience: the right to appear and conduct proceedings in a court.

Settlor: also referred to as a trustor or donor. This is the person who settles his property on someone, in particular to set up a trust.

Solicitor: is a legal professional within the English system. A solicitor has four main areas of competence: conveyancing, probate, drafting company and commercial contracts and the preparation of litigation. Unless he has an advocacy certificate, his right to be heard in court is in general limited to the lower courts.

State courts: this is the term given to the courts in the individual states of the USA as opposed to the courts in the federal system.

Statute: a form of written law, such as an Act of Parliament, passed by a legislative body.

Statutory instrument: subordinate or delegated legislation, usually made by a minister, under the authority granted by an Act of Parliament.

Superior: this adjective is applied to courts of higher jurisdiction. Precedents set in the superior courts must be followed by the lower courts.

Trust: property, either land or personal property, that is held by one party for the benefit of another party. Property held in trust comprises two interests: a legal interest and an equitable interest. The legal interest is held by the **trustee** and the equitable interest is held by the **beneficiary**.

Trustee: person who holds the legal title to property which is administered for the benefit of someone else.

US Bankruptcy Court: only the federal courts may hear bankruptcy cases.

US Claims Court: a federal court hearing claims against the USA.

US Court of International Trade: specialised in cases involving international trade.

US Supreme Court: this is the top court in the federal court system of the USA.

US Tax Court: a federal court hearing tax cases.

Voir dire: see **jury vetting**.

LEGAL SYSTEM DISCUSSION QUESTIONS

1. What are, in your opinion, the advantages and disadvantages of:
   * coded systems of law;
   * traditional common law systems?

2. Do you think it is a good idea to have a uniform legal profession as in the USA or a split profession such as in England?

3. Is it useful to have a system of binding precedent?

4. Is jury trial the best way to try cases?

LEGAL SYSTEM KNOWLEDGE QUESTIONS

1. Some courts are of a higher status than others. Give two general terms which can be used to indicate more important courts.

2. What are **magistrates** in the English court system?

3. What is meant by the term **forum shopping?**

4. What alternatives are available for a case to be tried other than in a mainstream court of law?

5. Name the two types of practicing lawyer in the English legal system. In what ways are their functions different?

6. What does the English term **jurisprudence** mean?

7. Explain the term **binding precedent**. This term is also known by a Latin term. What is this Latin term?

8. If a judge agrees with the decision reached by the majority of the other judges, he is said to what? What term is used to describe a judge's opinion which does not agree with the majority?

9. What is **statute** law?

10. What is meant by the term **equity** in the sense of a system of law?

2 Civil procedure terminology

In a civil dispute, lawyers will often try to help their clients reach an agreement with the other party in order to avoid going to court. However, if the parties to a dispute cannot reach agreement, the lawyers will prepare the case to be heard by a judge. Standard procedures must then be followed. These procedures are governed by civil procedure law.

It is quite possible that you will have to explain in English to a client what happens now. Your client will probably want to know what action you will take, the kind of information he must give you, and which court will hear his case. Finding a good English translation for a particular procedure in your own country is not always easy. To help you, this chapter describes civil procedure in the common law system.

2.1 Characteristics of civil procedure in a common law system

There are several major differences between the usual form of civil procedure in common law jurisdictions and that in many civil law systems.

* Traditionally, common law civil procedure has shown an **adversarial** approach to **litigation**. This means that it is the advocates who are responsible for finding and presenting evidence, and for arguing their clients' case in court. For example, examining witnesses should be done mainly by the lawyers, not by the judge. The judge listens and evaluates the evidence put forward by the lawyers, he may ask questions if something is not clear, but he does not take an active role in the inquiry himself. He acts as an umpire. This adversarial

approach has developed because a court case was always played out in front of a jury. It was the lawyer's task to convince the jury his client was in the right.

• Again because of trial by jury, much of the trial was conducted orally. It is still very important for trial lawyers to speak well, as oral presentation, as well as written arguments, are an important part of a trial. In England, only a very few civil cases are now tried by a jury. Nonetheless, civil procedure is still geared up to having a jury present. In the USA, litigants still have the right to jury trial for civil actions.

2.2   Up-dated civil procedure terminology in England

A few years ago, civil procedure underwent a reorganisation in England. Important changes were made and a new set of rules was developed. The aim of these new rules was not only to simplify civil procedure but also to make proceedings less adversarial and more efficient. These civil procedure rules have had a considerable impact upon the terminology of English civil procedure. Certain very old-fashioned terminology has been done away with.

> *N* Note: there has been no such reorganisation in the USA. This means that some of the old terms that have now gone in England are still used in the USA. For example, the one bringing a claim is stilled called the plaintiff in the USA, whereas England now uses the more modern term claimant. You should bear this in mind if your client is American. For this reason, major differences in terminology are pointed out below.

2.3   Civil procedure in England

As in civil law systems, in England the lower courts hear cases that are not very complicated and where the sums of money involved are not very great. The higher courts hear the more difficult cases and those where larger sums of money are concerned. To decide which case will go to which court there is a so-called tracking system. There are three tracks:

1. **Small claims track**: for cases less than £5,000.
2. **Fast track**: for most cases less than £15,000.
3. **Multi-track**: for most cases over £15,000.

The High Court, for example, is a senior court and will only hear the multi-track cases.

2.4 Starting a civil action

Take the following case. After years of saving, Mrs Smith has enough money to have a central heating system installed in her house. She agrees to pay Plumbing Cowboys Ltd £900 to install the system. When the system has been installed, it does not work. Annoyed by the attitude of Plumbing Cowboys Ltd, Mrs Smith asks an expert to look at the system. He says that the workmanship is so poor, and the central heating system so defective, that it will cost £500 to put it right. Mrs Smith then informs Plumbing Cowboys Ltd that she will not pay it a penny. Plumbing Cowboys Ltd decide to take Mrs Smith to court.

We will now follow the progress of the case as it makes its way through civil procedure.

The claimant
When a person decides to have his case heard by a court, he is said to bring a **civil action** (or **sue** the other party). The one bringing the action is called the **claimant**. In our case, Plumbing Cowboys Ltd is the claimant.

N Note 1: in some cases there is more than one claimant, as more people have suffered harm. If several claimants bring an action together, this is called **joinder of parties**.

N Note 2: sometimes, a very large number of claimants are involved. For example, where thousands of people have used a medicinal drug that turns out to have very serious side-effects. Rather than having many separate court cases, a representative action may be bought. In a **representative action**, the claimant is representing not only his individual interests, but also the interests of those who have been similarly affected. The American **class action** is based on this model.

In England, however, a **group action** is more common than representative action.

Filing the claim

To bring an action, a claim must be filed in the right court (depending on which of the three tracks your claim is on). It is also necessary to file the right sort of form in order to start a civil action. In England, most civil actions begin by filing a document called a **claim form**. The client must inform you properly about his case. He must tell you about the relevant facts of the case and the remedy that he wants. These details are put in the **particulars of claim**. The particulars of claim may be on the claim form itself or in a separate document. In our case, Plumbing Cowboys Ltd will explain that it has installed a central heating system at the request of Mrs Smith and it wants to be paid the £900 that was agreed.

The claimant or his lawyer must sign a **statement of truth**, verifying that the claim is a truthful one. Proceedings begin once the claim form has been issued by the court. It must be **served** on the other party. Various modes of service are permissible, for example a bailiff could deliver the claim form to Mrs Smith in person or it could be sent via the post.

2.5 Defending an action

The one against whom the claim is made is called the **defendant**. If Mrs Smith wants to fight the claimant's case, she must serve a document called a **defence** within a certain time. If she does not file a defence, there will be **judgment in default**. That means that the judge will find for Plumbing Cowboys Ltd without having heard what Mrs Smith has to say.

The defence should give details of the defendant's case. Mrs Smith must state in her defence that the workmanship was poor and the heating system does not work, which is why she refuses to pay the sum of £900. The claimant can file a **reply** to the defence.

Set off

The defendant may have a defence of **set off**. The defendant claims he is owed money by the claimant, which he intends to set off against the claimant's claim. In our case, Mrs Smith's lawyer has advised her not to pay any of the £900. Another lawyer may have proposed a different course of action: a set off. Plumbing Cowboys Ltd wants £900, but against that amount a sum of £500 should be set off, as that is the sum of money necessary to repair the heating system. That would mean Plumbing Cowboys Ltd could only recover, at most, £400 from Mrs Smith.

Counterclaim

A **counterclaim** is where the defendant brings a claim of his own against the claimant. For example, Mrs Smith could claim that because of the faulty heating system it was so cold in the house that she got frostbite in her toes. As Mrs Smith is a dancing teacher, she was not able to work for many weeks and has lost part of her income. She wants to bring a claim of £5,000 against Plumbing Cowboys Ltd for her loss of income and her pain and suffering.

2.6   Statements of case

The term **statements of case** refers to all the documents that are sent between the parties, like the claim form, the defence, or any reply to the defence.

N] Note: the term statements of case is quite new. The old English term for this was **pleadings**. The USA still uses the term pleadings.

2.7   Summary judgment

In England, either a claimant or a defendant can apply for a **summary judgment**. This procedure is relatively quick. It enables a judge to **strike out** either the whole claim or defence or part of it. If the whole claim or defence is dismissed, the case ends here and judgment is given immediately either in favour of the claimant or the defendant. It allows a judge to dismiss weak cases without wasting time when it is clear that either the claimant or the defendant has no real chance of success at trial.

> _N_ Note: the term **summary judgment** illustrates how difficult it can be to use terminology from a different legal system. For example, the term summary judgment is often used to translate a particular type of procedure in Dutch civil procedure, the so-called 'kort geding'. It is not a perfect translation. In Dutch law a case that has been heard at 'kort geding' could go on to be heard at a full trial. In English law, summary judgment means the end of the case because the case has been dismissed. Nonetheless, it is a useful translation because in practice most cases in the Netherlands do not go to trial once a decision has been made at 'kort geding'.

2.8   Settlement

Courts are very much geared up to promoting **settlement**. In a settlement, parties avoid going to trial by reaching agreement on the claim. This will save time and money. Either the claimant or the defendant may make a payment into court or an offer to settle at any time after the start of proceedings. For example, in our case Plumbing Cowboys Ltd could offer to pay the extra money needed to put the heating system right. Or Mrs Smith could offer to pay part of the £900. If the other party accepts, then there is no need to continue with the court proceedings.

2.9 Other pre-trial activities

In the common law system, there is a sharp distinction between procedures that take place before the trial and the trial itself. This is because the civil procedure was designed with a jury in mind. For example, this is why documents that a party intends to rely on at trial must be disclosed to the other party and the court before the trial itself.

2.9.1 Case management conference

A **case management conference** gives the judge an opportunity to make sure that the claim is clear, that the issues in dispute have been identified and that all agreements that can be reached between the parties about the issues involved have been reached. The judge gives directions and fixes a date for the trial.

2.9.2 Disclosure of documents

In English and American proceedings, before the trial itself each party has to draw up a list of all the documents they are going to use in the trial. This list must be served on the other party. For example, in our case one of the documents Mrs Smith will have to list is a letter from her expert setting out all the defects in the heating system. Each party has the right to ask for copies of the opponent's documents. This process is called **disclosure**. In this way, each party can determine before the trial the basis on which the other party will argue his case.

Your client may not have the right to see all the documents on the list, because some documents may be protected. A document could be covered by **privilege**. For example, the other party may not see a confidential letter between Mrs Smith and her lawyer. Documents may also be covered by **public interest immunity**.

N Note: in the USA this process of disclosure is called **discovery**.

2.9.3 Interim remedies

A long time can elapse between when a claim is first filed and when the judge finally hears the case. Sometimes, therefore, **interim remedies** may be ordered. Interim remedies include:

- **Interim payment**: this is a payment made before the trial to a person claiming money. In this way, it is possible to prevent hardship to a claimant, as the length of time between starting a civil action and the final judgment can be considerable.
- **Freezing injunction**: this stops a party removing or disposing of assets before trial. This is meant to prevent the situation arising that even if the court finds for the claimant, the defendant no longer has any assets available to pay the claimant's award. In the USA this is called **attachment**.
- **Interim injunctions**: a temporary court order requiring a person to do something or prohibiting a person from doing something until the end of the trial.
- **Search order**: this authorises someone to search and seize items and documents relevant to the claim or the defence, if there is a real danger that the other party would otherwise conceal or destroy that evidence.

2.9.4 The collection of written evidence

Before the trial, both parties collect written evidence.

- This evidence is usually in the form of a **witness statement**. A witness statement is the equivalent of the oral evidence which that witness would give if called to give evidence at the trial. The witness making the statement writes down the facts of the case as he experienced them. A witness statement may be in the form of an **expert opinion**, where the witness involved is considered to be an expert in the field. For example, in our case Mrs Smith's expert would be asked to make a statement about the defects in the heating installation.
- A party may apply for an order for a person to be examined before the hearing takes place. The witness gives evidence before an examiner and he may be **cross-examined** as if it were the trial itself. The evidence so given is then written down and put into evidence at the trial. This evidence is referred to as a **deposition**. It is also more convenient to col-

lect the evidence this way if the witness lives in a different country from the one where the trial will be heard.

- Sometimes a witness has to give his written evidence in the form of an **affidavit**. Taking an affidavit is more expensive than an ordinary witness statement, as it is a statement sworn before an independent third party.

_N Note: even if a witness has given a written witness statement, he can still be summoned to appear in person at the trial. If a witness does not want to attend the trial, he can be compelled to come. In that case, a **witness summons** is issued. In the USA, the old Latin term for a witness summons is still in use, namely the term **subpoena**.

2.10 Trial

Civil law systems are more geared up to handling a case based on written documents. Long civil trials, with extensive oral presentations by the advocates, are unusual. In England, because cases used to be tried before a jury, it was normal to present evidence and arguments orally rather than using written **submissions**. Today, most trials are heard by judges without a jury. Nonetheless, trials tend to be conducted as if a jury was still present. The trial continues to be heard in a concentrated period of time, as it was when a jury had to be called together. Oral presentation has remained important, although the typical English trial has now become a mixture of oral and written submissions. A so-called **skeleton argument** is usually required from both parties. In this way, the judge knows in advance the main arguments the parties' lawyers will put forward at the trial itself.

2.10.1 The trial timetable

```
┌─────────────────────────────┐
│ opening speech by the lawyers: │
│          optional            │
└─────────────────────────────┘
              │
              ▼
┌─────────────────────────────┐
│  examination of the witnesses │
│  called to support the claimant │
└─────────────────────────────┘
       ╱               ╲
┌──────────────────┐   ┌──────────────────┐
│ examination-in-chief by the │   │ cross-examination by the │
│ claimant's lawyer │   │ defendant's lawyer │
└──────────────────┘   └──────────────────┘
       ╲               ╱
┌─────────────────────────────┐
│ re-examination of the claimant's │
│          witnesses           │
└─────────────────────────────┘
              │
              ▼
┌─────────────────────────────┐
│  examination of the witnesses │
│ called to support the defendant │
└─────────────────────────────┘
       ╱               ╲
┌──────────────────┐   ┌──────────────────┐
│ cross-examination by the │   │ examination-in-chief by the │
│ claimant's lawyer │   │ defendant's lawyer │
└──────────────────┘   └──────────────────┘
       ╲               ╱
┌─────────────────────────────┐
│ re-examination of the defendant's │
│          witnesses           │
└─────────────────────────────┘
              │
              ▼
┌─────────────────────────────┐
│  closing speech for the defence │
│  closing speech for the claimant │
└─────────────────────────────┘
              │
              ▼
         ┌──────────┐
         │ judgment │
         └──────────┘
              │
              ▼
      ┌────────────────┐
      │ order for costs │
      └────────────────┘
```

2.10.2 Evidence

There are four main types of evidence:
- **oral evidence**: this evidence is given by the witnesses during the trial. These days, evidence may be given to the court via a video link or even a telephone if a video link is not available. A witness must take an oath or make an affirmation that what he says is true. If a witness deliberately gives false evidence, he is guilty of **perjury**;

- **real evidence:** this covers evidence of a physical nature, for example in our case a faulty piece of piping;
- **documentary evidence:** this covers all evidence that falls under the definition of **document;**
- **circumstantial evidence:** evidence that can be inferred from the facts.

2.10.3 The burden and standard of proof

In general, the **burden of proof** falls upon the one who brings the claim. The claimant must be able to prove all the elements required for his claim. If he cannot, then the court must find for the defendant. There are certain circumstances in which the burden of proof may shift to the defendant, for example in a negligence claim (see Chapter 4 on tort).

The **standard of proof** in civil cases is lower than in criminal cases. Whereas in criminal trials the prosecution must prove the guilt of an accused **beyond a reasonable doubt**, in civil cases the standard is **on the balance of probabilities.**

> *N* Note: in the USA, the usual formula for the standard of proof in civil cases is a **preponderance of evidence.** (The formula for the standard of proof in criminal cases is the same as in England: beyond a reasonable doubt.)

2.11 Appeal

In England, if the judge has found against you, you need the court's **permission** to bring an appeal in a civil case. For example, if the court decides that Mrs Smith does not have to pay Plumbing Cowboys Ltd anything because it did not perform the contract properly, Plumbing Cowboys Ltd could ask for permission to bring an appeal. An appeal is normally heard by the next court up in the hierarchy. A court that can hear appeals may be referred to as an **appellate court.** The party bringing an appeal is referred to as the **appellant** (in our case Plumbing Cowboys Ltd) and the other party is the **respondent** (Mrs Smith).

Note 1: in the USA, the losing party usually has the right to one appeal, being an appeal to the next court in the hierarchy. The one bringing an appeal is referred to as the **appellant** and the one defending an appeal is referred to either as the **respondent** or as the **appellee**.

Note 2: there is a difference between **appeal** and **cassation**. Some countries, like the Netherlands, have both appeal courts and cassation courts. The Supreme Court of the Netherlands is a court of cassation. So what is the difference between appeal and cassation? Put simply, an appeal court acts as if the case had not been heard before. It hears disputes about the facts of the case or points of law or both. It may substitute its decision for that of the court of first instance. A cassation court deals with a point of law only. It does not review facts. If it thinks that a lower court misinterpreted the law, it must send the case back to the same or a different lower court, so that the case can be heard again, bearing in mind the decision on the point of law made in the court of cassation. The traditional model for this type of system was developed in France and this system has influenced a number of civil law systems.

2.12   Costs

It is a simple fact of life that litigation is expensive. The value of the claim to the claimant can be completely overshadowed by the costs of the action. Costs are awarded at the discretion of the court. In England, the so-called **cost-shifting rule** applies: whoever loses the case has to pay not only his own costs, but also the costs of the other side.

Note: this is not the case in the USA: the practice known as the **American rule** is that the parties pay their own costs, whether they win or lose. There are only a few exceptions to this rule.

Legal fees
If your client is poor, he may qualify for legal aid. English lawyers may now also enter into **conditional fee** agreements with their clients. This is similar to the 'no win, no fee' approach to litigation common in the USA.

Note 1: conditional fees are the English version of the American **contingency fees**. However, strict rules mean that the conditional fee system tends to be less advantageous to English lawyers than the American system of contingency fees.

Note 2: some countries do not approve of the 'no win, no pay' approach to paying legal fees. If that is the case in your country, you may have to explain to your client that payment on a contingency fee basis is not allowed.

2.13 Enforcement of judgments

A **judgment creditor** is the name given to the winning party, who has been awarded a money judgment by the court. This judgment is enforceable against the loser, the **judgment debtor**. In our case, if Plumbing Cowboys Ltd loses, it will be the judgment debtor. It will have to pay the legal costs of both parties and any money judgment that may be awarded to Mrs Smith. How does the winning party get his money?

Seizure of goods
If necessary, the court makes use of a **writ of execution** that authorises the sheriff to seize the goods of the debtor and to sell them. The judgment creditor is then paid his court award out of the proceeds of the sale. The debtor is only allowed to keep certain personal items and other items necessary for his work.

Third party debt orders
A **third party debt order** enables the judgment creditor to divert money that would normally have been paid by a third party to the judgment debtor. For example, the Plumbing Cowboy's bank can be ordered to pay the judgment debt to Mrs Smith out of the Plumbing Cowboy's bank account.

Note: the Americans still use the old terms **garnishment** and **wage garnishment** for these orders.

CIVIL PROCEDURE VOCABULARY

Adversarial proceedings: proceedings involving a real dispute between two opposing parties. These opposing parties are responsible for finding and presenting evidence.

Affidavit: a sworn written statement made by a witness.

American rule: is that the parties pay their own costs, whether they win or lose. There are only a few statutory exceptions.

Appeal: the losing party appeals to a higher court for a review of the decision reached by the lower court.

Appellant: the party bringing an appeal.

Appellate court: an appellate court acts as a court of second instance, hearing the issues afresh, whether of fact, or law or both. It may substitute its decision for that of the court of first instance. Note, however, that although reference is made to the term 'appeal' in the USA, the function of the American appellate courts more often resembles that of the civil law courts of cassation.

Attachment: in the American sense of the word it is a writ authorising seizure of property, which will be held until the final decision in the case at issue.

Burden of proof: in general, it is the claimant who must prove all the elements required for his claim against the defendant. If he cannot do so, then the court must find for the defendant.

Case management: the judge makes sure that the claim is clear, the issues in dispute have been identified and that all agreements that can be reached between the parties about the issues involved have been reached. At the **case management conference**, the judge gives directions and fixes a date for the trial.

Cassation: a court of cassation is only competent to make a decision upon a point of law. In the English system there are no courts of cassation, as the appellate courts have the right to hear issues of fact and law.

Civil action: where the lawsuit involves civil, private, law rather than criminal law.

Claim form: the usual way of commencing proceedings in England, replacing the former use of writs in the High Court.

Claimant: the one bringing an action in English proceedings is now referred to as a claimant. The old term 'plaintiff' is no longer in use in England.

Class action: is used in the USA to bring a lawsuit on behalf of a whole group of individuals who have been affected.

Conditional fee: the English version of the American contingency fee, which is based on a 'no win, no fee' approach to litigation.

Contingency fee: American term where the attorney has entered into an agreement with his client that he will only receive his fee if he wins.

Cost-shifting rule: English rule stipulating that whoever loses the case has to pay not only his own costs, but also the costs of the other side.

Counterclaim: a claim brought by a defendant in response to the claimant's claim in the same proceedings.

Cross-examination: questioning of a witness, by a party that has not called the witness, about statements made by the witness during the examination-in-chief.

Defence: document produced by the defendant in response to the claim form.

Defendant: the one against whom the claim is brought.

Deposition: prior to the trial itself, the witness gives evidence before an examiner and he may be cross-examined as if it were the trial itself. The evidence so given is then written up and put into evidence at the trial. This is called a deposition and the one giving evidence in this way is referred to as the **deponent**. In the USA it is not usually the case that an examiner will be present, just the party being examined and the lawyers.

Disclosure: in English procedural law standard disclosure requires the disclosure of any document that a party intends to make use of at trial. Standard disclosure is achieved by making a list of these documents available to the other party. This process was formerly referred to as discovery.

Discovery: the American term for disclosure.

Document: defined in English proceedings as anything in which information of any description is recorded.

Evidence: there are four main types of evidence: **oral evidence** given by witnesses during the trial; **real evidence** of a physical nature; **documentary evidence** and **circumstantial evidence**, which is evidence that can be inferred from the facts.

Examination-in-chief: is the term given to direct examination, where the advocate calls a witness to support his client's version of events.

Expert opinion: evidence given by a witness who is a specialist in a certain subject.

Fast track: this is the track used for claims for a value above that for small claims, but less than that for multi-track claims. It will usually be heard in the County Court.

File: a document is filed if it is delivered, by post or otherwise, to the court office. It may have to be **re-filed** if it was not submitted to the appropriate court.

Freezing injunction: order of an English court to stop a party removing or disposing of assets before trial.

Garnishment: term still used in the USA where a writ of garnishment allows the judgment creditor to seize the property of the judgment debtor which is in the possession of a third party.

Group action: where a number of individuals bring an action as a group.

Interim injunctions: an interim injunction is a temporary court order.

Interim payment: this is a payment made before the trial to a person claiming a money judgment.

Interim remedies: are discretionary and may be ordered any time after the court has issued a claim form. Interim remedies include interim payments, a freezing injunction, a search order and interim injunctions.

Joinder of parties: uniting parties in a single action, whether as claimants or defendants.

Judgment creditor: is the name given to the party who has been awarded a money judgment by the court.

Judgment debtor: the one against whom a money judgment has been ordered.

Judgment in default: where the defendant has failed to serve a defence within the required time.

Litigation: where a dispute is taken to court. The parties are then the litigants.

Multi-track: this track is for claims for a value higher than that specified for the fast track. A multi-track case will be heard either by the county court or the High Court.

Particulars of claim: may be on the claim form itself or served as a separate document. The particulars must contain certain information about the nature of the claim and the remedy required by the claimant.

Perjury: telling lies in court while under oath.

Permission: here used in English legal terminology to indicate that permission must be given before a civil case can be appealed. This is in contrast to the USA, where there is usually a right to appeal once.

Petition: means of commencing certain specialist proceedings such as an action to wind up a company.

Petitioner: the one submitting a petition.

Plaintiff: the term still in use in the USA to indicate the one bringing an action.

Pleadings: this word refers to all the documents exchanged between the parties setting out their claims and defences.

Privilege: the right of a party to refuse to produce documents or answer questions on the ground of some special interest recognised by law.

Public interest immunity: this allows a party not to disclose matters on the grounds that disclosure would be injurious to the public interest, for example with respect to matters of national security.

Reply: a document in which the claimant replies to the answers given by the defendant.

Representative action: this term is used in England where the claimant is representing not only his individual interests, but also those of others who have been similarly affected.

Respondent: when a case is appealed, the one bringing the appeal is called the appellant and the other party is called the respondent. A respondent is also known as an **appellee** in the USA.

Search order: authorises the representatives of the applicant to enter the defendant's premises for the purpose of searching and seizing evidence where there is a risk that it will be concealed or destroyed.

Seizure of goods: the court issues a writ authorising the sheriff to seize the goods of the debtor and to sell them to satisfy the judgment debt.

Service: documents used in court proceedings must be brought to the attention of the other party. The delivery, or service, of documents can take various forms, for example personal service on the defendant/claimant or via the post.

Set off: the defendant claims he is owed money by the claimant which he intends to set off against the claimant's claim.

Settlement: parties avoid going to trial by reaching agreement on the claim.

Skeleton argument: both parties have to set down in a written document a summary of the **submissions** to be put forward during the trial.

Small claims: claims of under a certain specified, relatively low value are allocated to the small claims track. It will be heard in the county court.

Standard of proof: this is lower in civil cases than in criminal cases. Whereas in criminal trials the prosecution must prove the guilt of an accused beyond a reasonable doubt, in civil cases the English standard is on the **balance of probabilities** and in America the usual formulation is a **preponderance of evidence**.

Statement of truth: a statement of truth is added to statements of case or a witness statement to verify that the contents of the statement are accurate and honest.

Statements of case: in England, this is the collective term for all the documents exchanged between the parties such as the claim form, particulars of claim, a defence and any reply to the defence. The old term was the 'pleadings'.

Strike out: to delete a claim, or cancel an action, for example, because the claim reveals no grounds for bringing an action.

Submission: an argument to be pleaded before the court.

Subpoena: in the USA a court order requiring a witness to appear in court. In England this term is no longer used and has been replaced by the term 'witness summons'.

Sue: to start legal proceedings to take someone to court.

Summary judgment: it enables a claimant or a defendant to obtain judgment on the whole claim or on a particular issue without going to full trial when it is clear that either the claimant or the defendant has no real chance of success at trial.

Third party debt order: new English term for a **garnishee order**. It enables the judgment creditor to receive money that would normally have been paid by a third party to the judgment debtor.

Third party proceedings: where a person other than the original claimant and defendant becomes an additional party to the proceedings. For example, where the defendant brings a claim against a person for a contribution or indemnification.

Trial: hearing of the issues in contention tried either by a judge alone or by a judge and jury. Common law trials are a mixture of oral and written submissions. Juries in civil trials are now rare in England, but usual in the USA.

Wage garnishment: American term indicating that a certain proportion of the judgment debtor's earnings is subject to garnishment. In other words, part of the judgment debtor's income will be paid to the judgment creditor.

Witness: person who gives evidence to the court either as to facts or in the form of an expert opinion.

Witness statements: whether as to facts or in the form of expert opinions these statements are prepared in a written form. The document states the evidence that the witness would give if he were called to testify in court.

Witness summons: witnesses can be compelled to attend a trial. This is the term now used in England but before the new rules, this summons was referred to by the Latin term **subpoena**.

Writ of execution: directed to the sheriff of the county. Writs of execution in the USA can be obtained against all types of property belonging to the judgment debtor, both real and personal, although some property is exempt.

CIVIL PROCEDURE CASE DISCUSSION

Sally books a skiing holiday in Austria with Messup Tours. The holiday was described in Messup Tours' brochure as being a fun house party arrangement. There would be a bar, a welcome party, a disco, a candlelight dinner, a fondue party, and après ski get-togethers. All the guests would speak English. Being a sociable person, Sally was really looking forward to her house party skiing holiday.

When Sally gets there, she finds that the bar is only open until 6.00 p.m. There are three other people in the house and none of them speaks English. That makes the welcome party rather boring. The disco planned for the next day is cancelled because there are too few people. Two days later, the other guests leave and Sally has to spend ten days on her own! Although she has enjoyed the skiing, the house party has been a disaster. Disappointed and annoyed, Sally decides to sue Messup Tours.

Describe the civil procedure that will now be followed.

CIVIL PROCEDURE KNOWLEDGE QUESTIONS

1. In the USA, the one bringing a civil action is generally called the **plaintiff**. What name is given to the one bringing a civil action in England?

2. In England, what is the usual document used to start a civil action?

3. What are **statements of case**? What term is used in the USA instead of statements of case?

4. Explain the difference between a **counterclaim** and a **set off**.

5. What is a **summary judgment**?

6. The English term **disclosure** and the American term **discovery** refer to what sort of pre-trial procedure?

7. Explain the term **freezing injunction**.

8. What is meant by the term **standard of proof**?

9. What is the difference between the **American rule** and the English **cost-shifting rule** with respect to costs?

10. What term is given in the USA to fees paid on a 'no win, no fee' basis? How is this referred to in England?

3   Tort terminology

In private law, individuals bring claims against other individuals. Private law is also referred to as civil law because it is the law used by citizens if they believe that their legal rights have been abused by other citizens. The law of tort is a major part of private law. Today the most important tort of all is the tort of negligence, where the negligence of the defendant has led to the claimant suffering harm. The defendant's careless behaviour could cause the claimant to suffer physical injury, mental injury or financial loss. It is because the law of negligence is so important for all those involved in the practice of law that this particular tort is the main subject of this chapter. A number of other torts are also looked at briefly.

65

3.1   What is the law of tort?

A **tort** is a civil wrong, rather than a criminal wrong. The civil law protects individuals against certain types of wrongful acts by others, if these acts cause them harm. A person will be liable in the law of tort if his wrongful conduct has breached those legally protected rights. But what sort of behaviour is wrongful according to the law? Some coded systems, like the Dutch Civil Code, have tried to define what kind of wrongful act will be seen as a tort (classed in Dutch as 'onrechtmatige daad'). However, the approach to the law of tort is quite different in the common law. There are no general principles as to what is wrongful behaviour. The English law of tort is rather a collection of different sorts of wrongful behaviour. The diagram below gives you an idea of some of the categories of behaviour considered to be wrongful behaviour by the English law of tort.

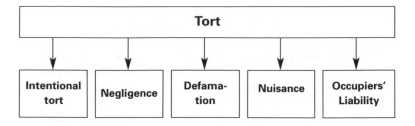

In English legal terminology, conduct is said to be **tortious** when a defendant has committed a specific tort. And each specific tort has its own rules to decide whether a defendant can be held responsible in law for his act or in some cases for his failure to act (an omission).

Note 1: in English law, there is a certain overlap between the law of tort and contract law. The major difference between the two branches of law is that with respect to the law of tort, the law has fixed what kind of behaviour is wrongful. With respect to contract law, the contractual agreement between the parties lays down what will be seen as wrongful behaviour. Liability for **breach of contract** (see Chapter 4) and tortious liability may, however, arise from the same facts.

Note 2: there is also a considerable overlap between the law of tort and criminal law, as many torts are also crimes, for example assault. However, the law of tort and the criminal law serve different purposes. The law of tort exists to give a personal remedy to individuals for any wrong they have suffered. Criminal law, on the other hand, is primarily concerned with the protection of the public at large and will punish offenders for socially undesirable behaviour.

Parties
The claimant or defendant in a tort case may be either a **natural person** or a **legal person**. A natural person is a person like you or me. A legal person is typically a registered company (see Chapter 5).
Sometimes the defendant in a tort case is not the one who actually carried out the wrongful behaviour, but the law holds him

responsible for the acts of the one who did cause the harm. For example, a parent can be held liable for the wrongdoing of a child. An **employer** can be held liable for the torts of an **employee**, if those torts were committed in **the course of employment**. This is called **vicarious liability**.

N Note: wrongful acts by an **independent contractor** do not, as a general rule, give rise to vicarious liability. The reason for this is that a contractor is self-employed and is therefore responsible for his own acts.

3.2   Negligence

If you have suffered harm, for example physical injury, because someone intentionally set out to hurt you, that person's behaviour will be seen by the law as wrongful. But what happens if you have been injured by someone who did not mean to hurt you? You were injured simply because that person did not take proper care. For example, you are hurt in a car crash because the other driver was driving at the same time as kissing his girlfriend. That driver's behaviour led to your injury. However, it was not his intention to hurt you, but he was **negligent**. The harm you suffered was his fault.

3.2.1   Requirements

In ordinary English, negligence is the word used to describe a careless act, or lack of attention, that causes harm to another. The English legal term **negligence** is far more specific. In order to succeed in a claim for negligence, a claimant must show that three requirements have been satisfied:
- The defendant owed him a **duty of care**.
- There was a **breach** of the duty of care.
- The harm suffered was **caused** by the breach of a duty of care.

Let us take the example of the kissing driver:

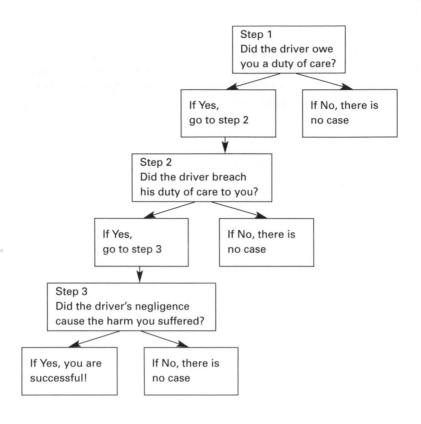

Duty of care

It is clear from the above diagram, that a claimant has no case unless he can show that the defendant owed him a **duty of care**. What, then, is a duty of care?

The test laid down in English law is called the **neighbour principle** because whether there is a duty of care depends upon whether the claimant is a neighbour in the legal sense of that word. A person is a 'neighbour' if what you do will directly affect him. For example, if you drive a car without taking proper care that could directly affect another road user. The other road users are then, in law, your 'neighbours'. A person is under a duty to take **reasonable care** to avoid acts or omissions, 'which you can **reasonably foresee** would be likely to injure your neighbour'. So if you could reasonably foresee that a lack of proper care could cause a person harm, you owe that person a duty of care.

Note 1: reasonable foreseeability is still the major test, although other factors may be taken into account. It could be the case that it is not fair to impose a duty of care on someone, for example because he is a fireman rushing along the road in order to save the lives of people in a burning building.

Note 2: certain duties of care have now been laid down in statute form. For example, there are also statutory duties of care that regulate an employer's liability towards his employees. Various statutes regulate specific aspects of health and safety.

Duty of care and nervous shock

Sometimes, the injury the claimant has suffered is not physical but mental. If a defendant is to be held liable for nervous shock, in other words mental injury, then injury by way of nervous shock must in itself be reasonably foreseeable. For example, due to his careless driving, a motorcyclist killed himself in an accident. A woman who did not see the accident because her view was blocked by a tram, but heard the noise and saw blood on the road, suffered nervous shock which caused her baby to be stillborn. It was held she could not claim for negligence because the motorcyclist could not have reasonably foreseen nervous shock to a person who had not directly witnessed the accident.

Note: it is not always clear from English case law when injury by way of nervous shock will be considered to be **reasonably foreseeable**.

Duty of care and financial loss

You want to invest in a company. The information published by the company shows that it is making a good profit. So you buy shares in the company. Unfortunately for you, the company had got its information wrong because it had not carried out a proper investigation. Its shares are hardly worth anything and you lose a lot of money. You have not been physically hurt by the company's negligence. But the company made a false statement, which you acted on, and because of that false statement you have suffered a financial loss. There is no contract between you and the company, as you bought the shares on the open market. Can you sue the company in tort? After all, the company was negligent and that negligence caused you financial loss.

A false statement in legal terminology may also be referred to as a 'misstatement' or, more specifically in the context of the tort of negligence, as a **negligent misstatement**. So when should a person be held liable in tort for negligent words that caused another financial loss? It would hardly be fair always to hold someone liable, for example a person may have made the statement while chatting at a party. If you are going to bring a claim, therefore, you will have to show that the defendant owed you a duty of care. To prove there was a duty of care, you will need to show:

- a **special relationship** between claimant and defendant. There is a special relationship where one party will trust what he has been told because the other party has special skill and expertise, for example you would trust the information given by a lawyer or an accountant; and
- because of this special relationship, the claimant could reasonably be expected to **rely** on the statement.

In our example you could argue that there is a special relationship between you and the company. The company produced a professional brochure apparently based on expertise. It is reasonable for you to presume that the company is knowledgeable about its own affairs, and in turn it is reasonable for the company to presume that potential investors like you will rely on that information.
With respect to financial loss caused by **negligent acts**, the general principle is that pure financial loss caused by a negligent act rather than a negligent statement is not actionable, as there is no duty of care for such loss. The main reason for this is to avoid open-ended liability.

Breach of duty
If it has been established that the defendant did owe the claimant a duty of care, the next step is for the claimant to show that the defendant **breached** that duty of care. The test for determining breach is **objective**. The standard is one of **reasonableness**; whether the defendant has acted as a **reasonable man** would have acted in the situation. So has the defendant failed to do something that a reasonable man would have done, or has he done something that a reasonable man would not have done?

N Note: the **burden of proof** is on the claimant, which means that the claimant must prove that the defendant was at fault. The claimant must show that the defendant did not act in a reasonable way. It can be very difficult for the claimant to prove that the defendant failed to take reasonable care. In such difficult cases, instead of the claimant having to prove fault, the defendant has to prove he was not negligent.

Causation
Even if the claimant can show that the defendant owed him a duty of care and he breached this duty, he must still show that the defendant caused his injuries. In order to establish **causation**, there must be a clear link between the claimant's loss and the way the defendant behaved.

3.2.2 The defence of contributory negligence

A claimant must be able to prove a duty of care, a breach of that duty and causation in order to be successful. However, even if the claimant has proved all that, the defendant could still have a defence: the defence of **contributory negligence**.

In this defence, the defendant argues that the claimant's injury was only partly caused by the defendant's conduct; the claimant himself is also at fault and therefore partly to blame for his own injury. Take the example of our kissing driver. Although the kissing driver was responsible for the car crash, the injuries you suffered were much worse than they would have been because you were not wearing a seat belt at the time. That makes you partly to blame for the extent of your injuries.

Contributory negligence does not mean that a claimant has no case (although in the past it did). He can still bring a claim, but the damages he can claim will be less, reduced by the extent to which he can be blamed for his injuries.

N Note: in the USA this defence is called **comparative negligence** (or comparative fault).

3.3   Intentional torts

In negligence, you have suffered harm because someone did not take proper care. An intentional tort, on the other hand, is one where the defendant has intentionally inflicted harm on the claimant. This harm could be either harm to the claimant's person or his property.

- It is a tort if the defendant has interfered intentionally with the claimant's person, for example where the defendant has hit the claimant. The main forms of intentional interference with the person are **battery**, **assault** and **false imprisonment**.
- Intentional interference with the claimant's property covers two situations: where the defendant has interfered with the claimant's personal property or his land. Land is called **real property**. **Personal property** is the term for property that is not land.

3.4   Product liability

Your mother has bought you an electric orange squeezer so that you can make juice. Unfortunately, the first time you use it, it explodes and you get nasty cuts in your face. What can you do? You could sue the manufacturer for negligence. However, you would have to prove that it was the manufacturer's fault, that the manufacturer had indeed been negligent. Proving fault is not always easy, so in recent years a new sort of **consumer protection** has appeared. Instead of bringing a claim of negligence, you could bring a claim under **strict liability**. Strict liability means that you do not have to prove that the manufacturer acted either negligently or intentionally.

In our example, this would mean that you would not need to show that it was the manufacturer's fault that the machine exploded. But you would have to show that:

- the product, in this case the orange squeezer, was defective (defective in the sense that it was not safe); and
- **causation** in that the defect in the product caused the damage you suffered.

N Note: the claimant's damages will be reduced if the defendant can show **contributory negligence**, in other words that the claimant did not take proper care in using the product.

3.5 Occupier's liability

If you invite someone into your house, or your place of business, you are liable for your visitor's safety. In general, an **occupier** owes a **duty of care** to all visitors. The basic test for whether a person is the occupier is whether he controls the **premises**. The duty of care means here that the occupier must take reasonable care to see that the visitors will be reasonably safe using the premises for the purpose for which they have been invited by the occupier to be there.

3.6 Nuisance

Private nuisance

Imagine that late every night, your neighbour starts to play his drums so loudly that it has become impossible for you to sleep. Or that your neighbour keeps hundreds of rabbits in a shed in his garden, but does not keep the shed clean. The smell is very unpleasant. If your neighbour refuses to listen to you, your remedy is to bring an action in **private nuisance**. This tort covers the situation where the defendant's behaviour interferes in an unreasonable way with the claimant's use or enjoyment of his land. The damage suffered by the nuisance must be **reasonably foreseeable**.

Public nuisance
Public nuisance is where a group of people suffer a nuisance, for example an oil tanker has leaked oil into a harbour and all the boats that were moored there are covered in oil. However, any such damage must be a **reasonably foreseeable** consequence of the nuisance.

3.7 Defamation

You own an apple pie factory. The local newspaper prints a story that your factory is dirty and that your workers urinate into the apple pies. As a consequence, no one wants to buy your apple pies anymore. The tort of defamation provides a remedy to both individuals and organisations where untrue, defamatory statements, made by another, have had a bad effect on their reputation. As a result of those **defamatory statements**, damage has been suffered. There are two categories of defamation: **slander** and **libel**. An action is based on libel where the defamatory statements are in a more permanent form, for example in writing. Slander is usually in the form of an oral defamatory statement.

3.8 Remedies in tort

Claims must usually be brought within a certain period of time; this is called a **limitation period**. The limitation period varies according to the claim. Claims brought after the specified time will not be heard as they are said to be **statute barred**.

The aim of compensation in tort is to restore the injured party to the position he would have been in if the tort had not been committed. The injured party is, however, under a **duty to mitigate**, which means he must do all that is reasonable to avoid making more losses than necessary.

3.8.1 Damages

One of the most common and important remedies in tort, as well as in other civil actions, is **damages**. This term is sometimes misused by foreign lawyers as they fail to see the distinction between damages and damage.

- 'Damage' means harm done: it does not become damages with an 's' if there has been more than one sort of harm done.
- 'Damages' means financial compensation awarded to the claimant for the injury he has suffered.

Misusing these two terms can cause confusion in sentences like 'Damages will be limited to the sum of £1,000 for the damages.'

3.8.2 Injunction

An **injunction** will not be awarded if damages would be an adequate remedy. However, in certain tort cases, an injunction is usually the remedy the claimant wants. Take for example a nuisance case, where the overgrown trees in the defendant's garden are blocking out the light from the claimant's garden and the rooms at the back of his house. The defendant could be ordered to stop causing the nuisance, which would mean he would have to chop down the trees.

TORT VOCABULARY

Assault: the defendant causes the claimant to believe he is going to commit a battery.

Battery: the defendant interferes with the claimant's person. There must be some form of aggressive contact between the defendant and the claimant's body, but physical injury is not necessary.

Breach of a duty of care: the party owing a duty of care has failed in the performance of that duty.

Burden of proof: obligation to prove facts. This burden is usually on the claimant but the burden can shift to the other party in certain circumstances.

Causation: there must be a link between the damage suffered by the claimant and the defendant's act or omission.

Comparative negligence: term used in the USA. The negligence of the plaintiff is compared to the negligence of the defendant. The plaintiff's damages will be reduced in proportion to the extent of his negligence.

Consumer protection: a consumer is someone not acting in the course of business. Consumer protection under the law of tort is particularly concerned with defective products that have caused harm to a consumer or his property.

Contributory negligence: term used in England. It is a defence to a negligence claim. The defendant shows that the claimant failed to take proper care and was therefore partly to blame for the injury he suffered. The damages the claimant can recover will be less.

Course of employment: that the employee was doing his job at the time the tort was committed.

Damages: this is an important and common remedy in tort and many other branches of civil law. It means financial compensation for the claimant for the harm suffered.

Defamation: where the claimant's reputation has been damaged by a published, defamatory statement.

Defamatory statement: a statement which has lowered the claimant's reputation in the eyes of 'right thinking people'.

Duty of care: a duty binding on one party to avoid acts or omissions, which could reasonably be foreseen as likely to injure the other party.

Duty to mitigate: where a party has been harmed by the tortious behaviour of another, he is nonetheless under a duty to ensure that his losses are no greater than strictly necessary.

Employee: an individual who has entered into or works under a contract of employment.

Employer: an employer may be held liable for torts committed by those who work for him according to a contract of employment.

False imprisonment: the defendant deprives the claimant of his liberty, for example he locks him up.

Independent contractor: does not work under a contract of employment but under a contract for services. An independent contractor is self-employed, and not an employee.

Injunction: a remedy that a claimant can ask for in a tort case. It is an order of the court directed at the defendant compelling him to stop doing something or to do something.

Legal person: this is an artificial, legal construct. An abstract entity, for example a registered company, is a separate person in law.

Libel: a form of defamation, where the defamatory statements are in a more permanent form, such as in writing.

Limitation period: a claim must be brought within a specified, fixed period of time. This period may vary from tort to tort.

Natural person: this is a human being rather than an artificial legal construct.

Negligence: in legal terminology, this is more than mere carelessness. It requires that the defendant has breached a duty of care owed to the claimant, and as a result the claimant has suffered harm.

Negligent act: pure financial loss caused by a negligent act rather than a negligent statement is not actionable.

Negligent misstatement: a false statement made negligently. In certain circumstances, a duty of care is imposed on the maker of a negligent misstatement.

Neighbour principle: in the tort of negligence, this principle helps to determine whether the defendant owed the claimant a duty of care. It states that 'you must take reasonable care to avoid acts or omissions which you could reasonably foresee would be likely to injure your neighbour'. A neighbour, in the legal sense, is a person who would be so closely and directly affected by your act that you should take him into account.

Nervous shock: where psychiatric harm has been suffered by the claimant.

Nuisance: in general, infringement of the claimant's use or enjoyment of his land, for example because of noise or smells.

Objective test: the test in negligence for breach of a duty of care is not whether this particular defendant has acted unreasonably, but whether a reasonable person would have acted in this way.

Occupier: if a person controls premises, he is considered to be the occupier and as such owes a duty of care to all visitors. In certain circumstances this duty is owed even to persons who are not invited visitors.

Personal property: property other than real property, for example paintings, furniture or jewellery.

Premises: this word refers to the land and any buildings or structures on that land.

Private nuisance: where the defendant has interfered in an unreasonable way with an individual's use or enjoyment of his land.

Product liability: under consumer protection law there is strict liability for defective (i.e. not safe) products causing damage to consumers. Damage must be in the form of death, personal injury, or damage to other private property. The claimant must still prove that the product caused the damage.

Public nuisance: where the harm is to a group of members of the public. To bring an action for public nuisance, an individual must show that he has suffered special damage.

Real property: land and structures attached to the land.

Reasonable care: whether the defendant took reasonable care to prevent harm to the claimant is judged on the facts of the case.

Reasonable foreseeability: in a negligence claim, a major factor that must be taken into account in establishing a duty of care is whether the defendant could reasonably foresee that his behaviour would lead to the claimant being injured.

Reasonable man/person: the test for determining whether there has been a breach of a duty of care is objective. The standard is one of **reasonableness**; whether the defendant has acted as a reasonable man would have acted in this situation.

Slander: usually an oral defamatory statement.

Special relationship: there may be liability for a negligent misstatement if the nature of the relationship between the claimant and the defendant is such that the defendant could expect the claimant to **rely** on the statement.

Statute barred: if a claim is not brought within the fixed period available for that particular action, the claimant loses his right to bring his case to court.

Strict liability: the defendant has neither acted negligently nor intentionally, but he is still held liable. In tort, an area of strict liability both in the USA and England is that of consumer product liability.

Tort: is a private or civil wrong, resulting from a breach of a legal duty. The law of tort is a collection of different sorts of torts, as there is no general principle of liability for causing harm to another person.

Tortious: is the adjective referring to tort, hence 'tortious liability'.

Vicarious liability: where one person is held responsible for the wrongdoing of another person. For example, where an employer is held liable for the torts of an employee committed in the course of the employee's employment.

Tort case discussion

Mary owns a stable where she gives riding lessons. She has employed John to work as a stable boy. Unfortunately, John knows nothing about horses and is also very lazy.

Because he knows nothing about horses, John is responsible for letting one of the wilder horses escape. At the time the horse escapes, an old lady is walking along the road that runs past the stables. She is startled by the horse galloping at full speed towards her. The old lady falls and breaks her arm.

Because he is lazy, John has allowed a huge quantity of horse manure to build up at the back of the stables. The manure stinks terribly and the family that lives at the back of the stables is very angry.

- Explain to the old lady what her legal position is.
- Explain to the family what can be done to stop the smell.

TORT KNOWLEDGE QUESTIONS

1. Explain what is meant by the term **vicarious liability** in tort.

2. In the law of negligence, what is meant by **duty of care**?

3. In what circumstances has the defendant **breached** his duty of care to the claimant?

4. If a manufacturer of a product is held **strictly liable** for a defect in a product, what does that mean?

5. What is the name given to a defence to a negligence claim, where the defendant claims that the claimant is partly to blame for his own injury?

6. If someone has committed the tort of **nuisance**, what kind of wrongful behaviour is involved?

7. What is the difference between **real property** and **personal property**?

8. The tort of **defamation** covers two categories of defamation. What are these two categories and in what way do they differ?

9. When is someone considered to be the **occupier** of premises?

10. What are the two major **remedies** in tort?

4   Contract law terminology

CONTRACT LAW TERMINOLOGY IN CONTEXT

The international language of business is English. That means that the international language of contracts is English. So it is very likely that you will have to explain the contract law of your own country to a foreign client in English.

Your client may ask you various questions, such as:

- Is there a contract?
- Can he force the other party to carry out his side of the agreement?
- Can he be sued by the other party because he delivered the goods a day too late?

Clients will constantly want to know what their legal position is. This chapter deals with the kind of terminology that you will need to be familiar with in order to explain your contract law to them. But be aware: English and American contract law differs in some important ways from some of the general principles of contract law of civil law systems.

4.1   A culture clash: contract law in the common law system and the civil law system

There is something of a culture clash between the English law of contract and contract law in civil law systems. Lawyers in civil law systems tend to find English contract law harsh and inflexible. And English lawyers find the contract law of their continent neighbours far too vague. Why?

English contract law takes the line that an ordinary adult is perfectly capable of understanding a contract and if there is something he does not understand, or does not like in that contract, he should never have signed it. In a civil law system, like in the Netherlands, the courts are more likely to look at a contract from the point of view of what would be fair and reasonable between the parties.

4.2   Is there a contract?

Not all agreements are contracts. For example, a boy could agree to go out with a girl on a date. But that is not a contract. A **contract** is a specific type of agreement. It is an agreement between two or more parties that is **binding** in law, in other words, it is a legally enforceable agreement. This means that the agreement generates **rights and obligations** that may be enforced in the courts. So if the boy stands the girl up, she cannot sue him: a non-contractual agreement may impose a moral obligation, but no legal sanctions are available.

Most contracts do not have to be written (imagine how annoying that would be if every time you wanted to buy something, you had to enter into a written contract first). The term **simple contract** is used to describe a contract that does not have to be in any particular form. A simple contract may, nonetheless, be in writing. This is not because it is a legal requirement, but because a written agreement provides better evidence of what was agreed between the parties than an oral agreement.

However, some contracts are only binding if in a certain form: a written form. For example, a **deed** (a written document, signed by the parties and witnessed) is necessary to transfer the legal ownership of a house from one party to another. A contract that is not in the required form will be invalid.

4.2.1   Formation of a contract

If an agreement is to be in the form of a contract, Anglo-American law demands that certain basic elements must be present. For the formation of a contract, three elements are necessary:

1. **offer** and **acceptance**;
2. **intention** to create a legally binding relationship;
3. **consideration**.

Offer and acceptance

To make a valid contract, there must be agreement between the parties to the contract. What is offered must be accepted otherwise there is no contract.

Offer

The word **offer** has a very specific meaning in legal English, and that meaning is somewhat different from the ordinary English use of the word offer. If you get an advertisement through your letterbox, it may 'offer' you something, for example a crate of beer for £1. That 'offer' is not an 'offer' in the legal sense of the word. In legal terminology, an offer is a statement of willingness by the offeror to enter into a contract if the other party accepts all the terms of the offer. In the case of the crate of beer, the **offeror** would have to know how many crates you want and when you want them for it to be a binding offer. This is why in English law advertisements, such as price lists, are not offers in the legal sense of the word.

An offer is terminated when it has been **revoked**, or it has **lapsed** or been met with a **counter-offer**. If an offer has been revoked, this means that the offeror has taken back his offer. He can withdraw an offer any time before the other party has let him know he wants to accept his offer. The offeror must, however, tell the other party he is withdrawing his offer. An offer is said to lapse after the time limit for the offer has expired or, if there was no time limit, after a reasonable interval. It is also terminated where the **offeree** (the party to whom the offer has been made) does not accept all the terms of the offer and makes a counter-offer instead (this is explained in the next section).

Acceptance

Acceptance means that you let the offeror know that you accept all the terms of the offer unconditionally. If you want the offer to be changed in some way, for example you want to pay less money, this is not acceptance. Acceptance is only when all the terms of the offer are agreed to. In fact, if you propose a change to the terms of the original offer, you are actually making a new offer. This is called a **counter-offer**. A counter-offer is a rejection of the original offer and there can be no contract until the counter-offer is in turn accepted. For example, if the seller offers to sell his car for £6,000, but you are only prepared to pay £5,500, the £5,500 is a counter-offer. The seller now has a choice: as you have rejected his original offer of £6,000, he can revoke that offer and take the car back home; or he can decide to accept your new offer of £5,500, which means you now have a contract for the car.

> [N] Note: in negotiations, you may experience a number of offers and counter-offers.

Intention to create legal relations

Not all agreements are intended to create legally enforceable rights and obligations. Some agreements are only informal. If it can be shown that it was not the intention of the parties to create a legally binding relationship, then there is no contract. So how can you prove that you intended, or did not intend, to make a binding contract?

English law makes a **presumption** about your intentions. It presumes that if the agreement is with family or friends, the agreement was not intended to be binding. For example, your father promises to buy you a car if you stop smoking for a year. You take up his offer, but at the end of the year your father laughs and says he did not really mean it, he just wanted to give you the right incentive to quit smoking. Can you sue him for the car? Unless you can come up with some pretty strong evidence that this agreement was intended to be legally binding, the court will presume it was not meant to be.

In the case of commercial agreements, the presumption works the other way round. It is presumed that there *is* an intention to create a legally binding relationship. Again you would need very clear evidence to persuade the court that there was no intention to create legal relations.

Consideration

In the common law, **consideration** is a vital element in the formation of a contract. If there is no consideration, there is no contract. Unlike in civil law systems, the court only enforces a bargain, not a one-sided promise. In other words, in English and American law, in order to have a contract you must do something for me and I must do something for you. But if I do something for you and you do nothing for me, there is no consideration. That is why a promise to make a gift is not seen in English law as a contract because there is only consideration from the one promising to give the gift. The one who is to receive the gift promises nothing. The best way to make a gift, if you want to make it legally enforceable, is in the form of a **deed**.

So what is proper consideration? Typically, consideration is an exchange of promises to perform acts in the future. For example, a promise to deliver a bed in return for a promise made by the other party to pay for the bed. Is there only proper consideration if what you get from me is the same value as what I get from you? The answer to that is no. For example, if you have freely agreed to let me rent your flat for £1 per month, even if the ordinary market rate for renting that flat would be £100 per month rather than £1 per month, the consideration is sufficient. The courts will not defeat a contract simply because one of the parties has made a bad bargain.

4.2.2 Capacity

As in civil law systems, there is also no contract if one of the parties to the contract did not have the **capacity** to enter into a contract. This could be because one of the parties was a **minor**, in other words a child. Children are protected by the law from entering into unfavourable transactions. Most adults do have capacity, but not if they are of unsound mind. It should also be borne in mind that companies do not have the same capacity as you or me; for example, we could enter into a marriage contract, a company cannot. There are more restrictions on companies (see Chapter 5).

4.3 Breaking off contractual negotiations

In legal systems where the doctrine of **good faith** is recognised, breaking off contractual negotiations may give rise to legal consequences. The Italian Civil Code, for example, expressly states that there is a duty to negotiate in good faith. In the Netherlands, where the concept of reasonableness and fairness also plays an important role, once negotiations have clearly gone beyond an initial stage, the party that breaks off the negotiations may have to pay the costs of the other party and, if the negotiations have reached an extremely advanced stage, breaking off negotiations may no longer be allowed.

There is, in general, no duty to negotiate in good faith in English law. There is no liability, either in contract or in tort, for pulling out of negotiations at any stage and for whatever reason. If you have dealings with English lawyers, you should be aware of this.

> [N] Note: some other common law jurisdictions, such as the Australian and American, show more respect for the concept of good faith. The American UCC (see Chapter 1) imposes a duty of good faith and recent Australian case law indicates a development in that direction.

4.4   Parties to the contract

The general rule is that you only get the rights from a contract, or have to fulfil the obligations of a contract, if you are a party to the contract. If you are not a party, you can neither sue on that contract or be sued because of the contract. This is called the doctrine of **privity of contract**.

The strict rule has various exceptions to it. For example, imagine that you have entered into a contract with an insurance company. The aim of that contract is that your partner can benefit from the contract. It would make the contract totally pointless if the insurance company later refused to pay anything to your partner because she was not a party to the contract (as the contract was only between you and the insurance company). For this reason, English law allows a named or designated **third party** who is to benefit from the contract to enforce it.

4.5   The contract

If it is clear that there is a contract between the parties, it is then necessary to examine the contents of the contract. A contract consists of the promises that the parties have made to each other. These promises are legal obligations and are legally enforceable.

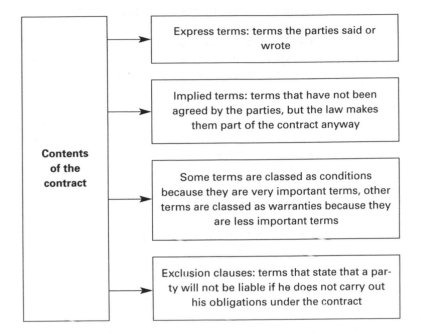

4.5.1 Classification of contract terms

A **term** is a promise that is a part of the contract. The importance of a contractual term can vary: it may be of fundamental importance, going to the very heart of the contract, or it may be of only minor importance. In English law, the terms of a contract are classified either as **conditions**, which are fundamental terms of a contract, or as **warranties**, which are minor terms.

Condition
A **condition** is a fundamental term. Its performance is so important that if the other party does not carry it out, you not only have the right to claim damages, but also to treat the contract as **terminated** (brought to an end).

Note: when drafting a contract, if a lawyer wants to show that a term is fundamentally important he may say that it is a condition.

Sometimes, instead of using the word condition, the lawyer will say that an obligation is **of the essence**. In this way, the lawyer is letting you know that if you do not carry out this term of the contract, his client will not only sue for damages, but will also have the right to terminate the contract with you.

Warranty

The word **warranty** is used to indicate that a term in the contract is of lesser importance. A warranty is a term that does not deal with the main purpose of the contract. That is why if you have not carried out your obligations under a warranty, the other party only has the right to sue you for damages, but not to terminate the whole contract.

> [N] Note 1: you will also find the word **warranty** used in several other ways. For example, it is commonly used in the sense of **guarantee**: the product has a **warranty** for a period of one year.

> [N] Note 2: in the USA, the term warranty is found used in the context of the sale of goods. If the seller has told you something about the goods, or implied something about the goods, what he has told you becomes part of the contract of sale. It is said to create a warranty. If the goods do not conform to what he told you, then you can bring an action against him for breach of warranty.

Express terms

Express terms are terms that the parties have specifically agreed to, being terms the parties either said or wrote. Sometimes when a lawyer drafts a contract, he calls an express term a 'condition'. That does not mean that the court has to accept that classification of the term. Even if a term has been described as a condition, the court can decide that it is really only a warranty.

Implied terms

English common law presumes that individuals can take care of their own interests. It is, therefore, not the job of the courts to sort out a contract by inserting new terms into it. Their task is only to interpret those terms that exist already. Nonetheless, English law does recognise that terms can be implied into a contract in certain situations.

In particular, **implied terms** are important in contracts for the sale of goods. Imagine you buy a boat. The first day you go out sailing, your boat sinks. When you complain to the seller, he says the contract did not promise that the boat would float, so bad luck. Do you have to accept that? Absolutely not! One of the terms implied into a contract of sale is that goods are of satisfactory quality and are fit for their purpose. The purpose of a boat is to float on water, so even though the contract did not state it would float, it is an implied term that it will float.

Most implied terms are conditions. These implied terms may not be **excluded** in a **consumer** transaction. Where the parties are not consumers, they may agree to exclude most of these implied terms, but only insofar as is reasonable (see next section).

4.5.2 Exclusion clauses

You have bought a new bed. When it is delivered, the mattress is absolutely filthy and stinks. When you complain to the shop manager, he tells you to read the contract. In the contract you see a term that says the shop will not be liable if the mattress is not in good condition. That term is called an **exclusion clause**. The purpose of an exclusion clause is to exclude all liability for failing to carry out the contract, either at all or not properly.

An exclusion clause is open to abuse. In order to prevent parties relying on **unfair contract terms**, there are strict legal rules about the use of exclusion clauses. The law protects consumers in particular against the wrongful use of exclusion clauses by businesses. We saw above that the law will imply certain terms into a contract in order to protect consumers. Similarly, in certain types of consumer contracts an exclusion clause will be **void**.

In our example, the mattress is not of satisfactory quality, so the shop cannot rely on its exclusion clause. Even if the parties to a contract for the sale of goods are **non-consumers**, the law on unfair contract terms still requires that the exclusion clause must be **reasonable**.

4.6   Ending the contract

A contract can come to an end either because it has been **set aside**, or it has been **discharged**.

A contract can be **set aside**, in other words cancelled, if it later appears there was something wrong with the contract. Misrepresentation, mistake, duress and undue influence are all reasons to have a contract set aside.

A contract is said to be **discharged** where the contract is perfectly valid, but it comes to an end because it has been carried out, or the parties agree to end it, or there is a serious breach of contract by one of the parties, or it is frustrated.

4.6.1   Reasons to have a contract set aside: vitiating factors

A contract may appear at first sight to be perfectly fine. However, it later appears that there is something wrong with the contract. This defect is so serious that you can have the contract **set aside** (the contract can be cancelled). A **vitiating** factor is the legal term given to a factor that can make a contract invalid. Misrepresentation, mistake, duress and undue influence are vitiating factors.

These vitiating factors can make a contract **void or voidable**. A void contract is one that was never legally valid or without legal effect. A voidable contract is one that can have legal effect but could be made void if you want to **rescind** it.

Misrepresentation

In negotiations leading up to the signing of a contract, representations are made. A **representation** is a statement that was made to encourage you to enter into the contract, but it does not itself become part of the contract. For example, you run a catering company and you are asked to put on a dinner for a big firm. You are told that Tom Cruise will be attending the dinner, so you agree to do it. When you sign the contract, the terms deal with the price of the dinner, the type of food, the place and date, but nowhere does it state that Tom Cruise will be attending the dinner. The part about Tom Cruise is not a term of the contract; it is only a representation.

After signing the contract, you find out that it is not true that Tom Cruise is going to be there. Can you pull out of the contract? The statement about Tom Cruise being there was false. In legal terminology, a **misrepresentation** is the name given to a false representation. Although you cannot bring an action for **breach of contract** (see below), because Tom Cruise being there was not a term of the contract, you can bring a special action for a misrepresentation if you would not otherwise have entered into the contract.

Remedies for misrepresentation

A misrepresentation makes the contract **voidable**. That means you can decide to cancel the contract, to have it set aside. You can claim rescission and/or damages.

- **Rescission**: if you **rescind** the contract, the clock is turned back. This means that the parties to the contract are put back in the position they were in before the contract was entered into. It is as if the contract never existed.
- **Damages**: in addition to, or as an alternative to, rescission, it is possible to sue for financial compensation if you have suffered any losses.

Duress and undue influence

At common law, a contract can be set aside if it was entered into under **duress** or **undue influence**.

- **Duress** means that either actual violence or the threat of violence was used to make the other party enter into the contract (such as, 'sign this contract or I'll shoot you!').
- **Undue influence** refers to improper pressure other than violence. For example, blackmail ('sign this contract or I'll tell your wife you are a homosexual').

Mistake

The legal term **mistake** has a far more restricted meaning than the ordinary English word mistake. Not all mistakes mean that a contract can be treated as non-existent. The old rule of **caveat emptor** (Latin for 'let the buyer beware') still applies in private sales where the parties are bargaining equals. For example, if you buy an 'antique' from a market stall, and then find out that it is not an antique but a modern copy, then caveat emptor will apply. Certain types of mistake will not make a contract invalid, for example, if you make a mistake about the time needed to carry out a contract.

However, if the mistake is absolutely fundamental, as it goes to the very heart of the transaction, the contract will be considered as **void** from the outset. For example, you hire Michael Jackson for your company Christmas party. You think you have hired the famous American singer. It turns out you have hired Michael Jackson, the singing barman from a pub in Dublin. That would be a fundamental mistake and would make the contract void.

4.6.2 Discharge of contractual obligations

Discharge means that you are released from an obligation. In contract law, it means the parties are free of their mutual obligations under the contract and, therefore, the contract comes to an end. The **termination** of a contract can be achieved in a variety of ways: by performance, express agreement, breach or under the doctrine of frustration.

Discharge by performance
The general rule is only when you have carried out everything you promised to do in the contract, exactly in the way you agreed to do it, will your contractual obligations be discharged. That is called discharge by **performance**, by having done exactly and precisely what you contracted to do.

Discharge by agreement
A contract may be **discharged by agreement** in several situations. The parties may have agreed that the contract should end automatically if some event occurs or after a fixed period of time. A contract is also said to be discharged if you and the other party agree upon a new contract that replaces the old one.

Discharge by breach
There will be **breach of contract** where a party:
- has made it clear that he will not carry out the contract; or
- has not performed his obligations properly.

Some breaches of contract will only give you the right to sue for damages, but not the right to terminate the contract. If the obligations have not been performed properly, whether you have the right to treat the contract as discharged by breach depends on whether there has been **fundamental breach** or not. That depends upon whether the term that has been breached is a **condition** or a **warranty**. For example, in the contract it states that you must deliver 10,000 tonnes of tomatoes on the 23rd of May. In fact you deliver the tomatoes two days later, on the 25th of May. If the date of delivery was a condition, the other party has the right not only to claim damages, but also to end the contract. That means he can refuse to take delivery of your 10,000 tonnes of tomatoes on the 25th of May. If the delivery date is a warranty, he does not have the right to refuse your tomatoes, only to sue you for any loss he might have suffered because you delivered two days late.

Notice of default
In some civil law systems, such as the Dutch and German, there is a legal obligation to give the other party **notice of default**. Before the other party is considered by the law to be in breach of contract, you must inform the other party that he has not performed his obligations. If performance is still possible, he is then given a fixed period of time in which to carry out his obligations. Only if he then fails to perform within that time will he be in breach.

In English law, if the other party has failed to perform on time, that is his responsibility. In general, you are not obliged to warn him he is in default or to give him time to put it right. Notice of default must be given, however, if this has been specifically agreed upon between the parties to the contract. An agreement to give each other notice of default is quite common commercial practice in common law jurisdictions.

[N] Note 1: in English law, you do not need to go to court to terminate a contract.

[N] Note 2: at common law, contractual liability for breach is strict and the motive for that breach is irrelevant. For example, if you have a bad cold and are not able to carry out your obligations under the contract at the agreed time, you will still be in breach even though it is not your fault that you came down with a bad cold. The court is not interested in why you did not carry out your obligation, nor whether you had tried your best to carry out those obligations.

The question is simply 'have you breached the contract or not?' In those civil law systems where fault plays a more significant role, this may seem a very harsh approach.

Discharge by frustration

You hire a room in a pub for your band to put on a show. Before the date for the show, the pub gets burned down. The fire is not your fault, nor is it the fault of the owner of the pub. Nonetheless, the fire has made it impossible to carry out the contract, as the room no longer exists. In these circumstances, the contract is ended. This is called **discharge by frustration**.

Sometimes it is not impossible to perform the contract, but events have so radically changed the situation that the contract has become a very different proposition to the one the parties thought they were entering into. For example, you book a hotel room expressly to watch the Queen's coronation ceremony. Unexpectedly, the Queen becomes ill and dies. The coronation is cancelled. Although the hotel room is still available, the whole purpose of the contract has been frustrated.

N Note 1: this doctrine of frustration is more usually referred to as the **doctrine of impossibility** in the USA.

N Note 2: it is usual for commercial contracts, whether common law or civil law, to include a **force majeure** clause. This clause includes a list of events considered to be outside the control of the parties, such as labour disputes, war, riot, compliance with a law or governmental order, accident, breakdown of machinery, fire or flood.

4.7 Remedies for breach of contract

If your client has been the victim of a breach of contract, he will want to know what the law can do to help him. There are various remedies available, depending on the facts of the case. Your client can put in a claim for damages if he has suffered loss. As we have already seen, if the other party refuses to carry out the contract, or if the breach is fundamental, he can also treat the contract as **discharged**.

Equity (see Chapter 1) also provides a number of remedies. Equitable remedies include **quantum meruit, specific performance** and **injunctions**. Equitable remedies are **discretionary**. They will only be awarded where damages are not a suitable alternative.

4.7.1 Damages

The legal term **damages** means financial compensation. The aim of damages in contract law is to put the claimant in the position he would have been in if the contract had been performed properly. Damages will compensate him for any loss suffered by the breach. Damages are designed to compensate you for the loss you have suffered. Nonetheless, an award of damages may include full **expectation damages** where appropriate. This means that a claimant may claim where he expected to make a profit on the contract, but he did not because the other party breached the contract. Damages should not, however, make a claimant better off than he would have been if the contract had been performed.

Liquidated damages and penalties

It is usually the court that decides how much will be awarded in damages. However, it may be that the parties themselves want to decide in advance how much should be paid if one of them does breach the contract. This is called **liquidated damages**.

- **Liquidated damages clause** is the name given to a term in a contract where the parties have made an honest attempt to estimate what their losses would be if one of the parties does not perform his obligations. If the court is convinced that the clause is a genuine estimate of loss, the court will enforce the clause.
- **Penalty clause** is the name given to a clause where one party intends to punish the other party for breach of contract, or deter him from defaulting, by making him pay a penalty. In a penalty clause the amount that has to be paid is much higher than the losses could really be. That is why an English court would ignore this clause and decide itself what a proper sum for compensation would be.

Remoteness of damage

The consequences of a breach of contract may be far-reaching. To prevent damages spiralling out of control, there must be a cut off point. The law says if the damages are too **remote** they cannot be recovered. So you could only sue me for damage that would **naturally arise** from the nature of the contract, for example, if I sell you a defective car, the costs of repairing your car naturally arise from my breach of contract.

If the losses do not naturally arise from the contract, in general they cannot be recovered. For example, if you miss a job interview because of the defective car, you cannot sue me for possible loss of earnings because I could not have reasonably foreseen you were going to a job interview. **Special notice** that that kind of loss could happen would have to be given to the other party.

4.7.2 Quantum meruit

Quantum meruit is Latin for 'as much as he deserves'. It arises in a situation where a contract has not been completely performed, but some work has been done under the contract and the claimant would like to be paid for that work. He asks to be paid 'as much as he deserves'. The claim can only be made where the other party voluntarily accepted **partial performance**, or where the claimant has been prevented by the other party from completing the performance of the contract.

4.7.3 Specific performance

Specific performance is an order to make a party perform his obligations under the contract.

N   Note: in the common law, you do not have the legal right to demand that the other party performs his obligations. Specific performance will only be ordered if damages are not a proper remedy. For example, the National Gallery has entered into a contract with John Bloggs to buy a particular painting by Renoir. That is a unique painting, so the National Gallery cannot buy it from anyone else. Then John Bloggs refuses to carry out the contract. Damages would not be an adequate remedy. In that case, the court could order John Bloggs to perform his obligations under the contract, which would mean ordering Bloggs to sell the painting to the National Gallery.

4.7.4 Injunction

With respect to contract law, an **injunction** is a court order to stop someone breaching a term of the contract. For example, a term of the contract states that neither party is allowed to disclose confidential information. If you think the other party is about to do just that, you do not want to be paid damages for your losses once that information is out in the open. What you want is to stop that information from being made public in the first place. You need an injunction that will stop the other party disclosing the information before it is too late.

4.7.5 Suspension of performance

In civil law systems, such as the French, German and Dutch, the principle of **exceptio non adimpleti contractus** generally applies: if the other party is in breach, you can stop carrying out your obligations under the contract. The law allows for **suspension of performance** in the event of breach.

N Note: that is not the case in the common law. There is no general principle allowing for suspension of performance if the other party is in breach. On the contrary, suspension of performance will in turn be breach of contract. There are, however, certain specific circumstances in which suspension is allowed. For example, in a sales contract non-payment by the buyer allows the seller to withhold delivery.

CONTRACT LAW VOCABULARY

Acceptance: this is the unconditional acceptance of all the terms of an offer.

Binding: an agreement between two or more parties that is binding in law is a legally enforceable agreement.

Breach of contract: the refusal or failure by a party to a contract to perform an obligation imposed on him under the contract.

Capacity: refers to the ability of a natural or legal person to enter into a contract.

Caveat emptor: Latin phrase meaning 'let the buyer beware'.

Condition: is a fundamental term of the contract. If it is breached, the innocent party may not only claim damages, but may also opt to treat the contract as ended.

Consideration: a contract must be a bargain. Each party gives value to the other by exchanging promises (or by a promise given in exchange for an act). This exchange of value is the consideration.

Consumer: a person not acting in the course of business. There are special rules that apply to contracts where one of the parties is acting as a consumer.

Contract: a contract is a legally enforceable agreement.

Counter-offer: if not all the terms of an offer have been accepted, then there is no acceptance of the offer, but a counter offer. This is in effect a new offer, which now has to be accepted by the other party.

Damages: in contract law, financial compensation that should put the claimant in the position he would have been in if the contract had been performed properly.

Deed: a written document that has been signed by the parties and witnesses.

Discharge: release from the obligations under a contract. Discharge may be by performance, agreement, breach or frustration.

Discharge by agreement: both parties agree to end the contract.

Discharge by breach: a contract may be discharged by breach where the party in default has refused to perform, or where the performance is so defective there has been fundamental breach.

Discharge by frustration: parties are excused from the contract if, through no fault of either party, after the formation of the contract it becomes impossible to carry out the contract or the contract has become commercially pointless.

Discharge by performance: the obligations under the contract have been carried out fully and exactly.

Doctrine of impossibility: term often used in the USA for the doctrine of frustration.

Duress: violence or threats of violence in order to make someone enter into a contract.

Exceptio non adimpleti contractus: Latin phrase referring to a principle in the civil law system, which allows the innocent party to suspend his own performance of the contract until the other party has carried out his obligations as agreed.

Exclude: to rule out liability for contractual failure.

Exclusion clause: term in a contract to exclude the liability of a party for contractual failure. That failure could be in the form of breach of contract, misrepresentation or negligence.

Expectation damages: damages you can claim in a breach of contract action, where the damages take into account the profit you should have received if the defaulting party had performed the contract as agreed.

Express terms: terms explicitly stated by the parties, either oral or written.

Force majeure: most contracts include a force majeure clause. This lists events considered to be outside the control of the parties and for which the parties cannot be held responsible.

Fundamental term/breach: a term is fundamental if it goes to the root of the contract. If it is breached, the breach is referred to as fundamental breach.

Good faith: negotiations and contractual relations should be characterised by honesty and fairness, by the intention to carry out the contractual obligations, and with no intention to seek an unfair advantage or purposefully act to the detriment of the other party. This principle is not operative in the common law of contract.

Guarantee: a legally enforceable promise that the goods are of good quality and will work properly. This is sometimes referred to as a warranty.

Implied terms: terms that can be read into the contract, either by custom, statute or by the courts.

Injunction: with respect to contract law, usually a court order to stop a clause in the contract from being broken. It is a discretionary remedy and will not be ordered if damages are a sufficient remedy.

Intention to create legal relations: there must be an intention to create a legally binding agreement.

Lapse: no longer valid. An offer is said to lapse when the time in which the offer could be accepted has expired.

Liquidated damages: where the parties themselves, rather than the court, have determined the level of damages.

Liquidated damages clause: a term in a contract where a proper attempt has been made to pre-estimate the loss that would result if the other party breaches the contract.

Minor: a minor is a person under the age of majority, the age of majority being eighteen years in English law.

Misrepresentation: where the representation is a false statement, it is called a misrepresentation. Misrepresentations can be fraudulent, negligent or innocent.

Mistake: where the mistake is of an operative and fundamental character, which goes to the very heart of the contract, the contract will be **void**.

Naturally arising: damages may be claimed for losses that arise naturally from the nature of the contract.

Non-consumer: a person acting other than as a consumer, carrying out some form of commercial activity.

Notice of default: notice is given to the defaulting party that he is in breach of contract, and a period of time is usually specified within which the defaulting party must fulfil his obligations. Notice is not a general requirement in English law, but parties are free to agree to give such notice.

Of the essence: words used in a contract to show that a particular term is of fundamental importance.

Offer: an offer shows a willingness to enter into a contract without further negotiations.

Penalty clause: the penalty is meant to punish the other party for breach, or deter him from breaching the contract. In English law, penalty clauses are in principle unenforceable.

Performance: to carry out obligations under a contract exactly and precisely.

Presumption: the law makes certain assumptions based on a set of facts. In order to override a presumption, a party must bring forward convincing evidence.

Privity of contract: a contract only confers rights and obligations on the parties to the contract. There are, however, exceptions to this rule, both in statute law and common law.

Quantum meruit: the claim of quantum meruit is for 'as much as he deserves'.

Reasonable: in order to prevent the abuse of exclusion clauses the law says such clauses must be reasonable. This also gives protection to non-consumers.

Remoteness of damage: the loss suffered by the innocent party must be either a natural cause of the breach, or the other party must have been informed that such a loss would occur because it is reasonably foreseeable by the parties as the probable result of a breach. If not, the damage is too remote and compensation cannot be claimed.

Representation: a statement that encourages a party to enter into the contract, but does not itself form a part of that contract.

Rescission: you can opt to have a voidable contract set aside. You are said to **rescind** the contract. Where there has been a misrepresentation, the contract can be made void and the parties are put back in the position they were in before the contract was made.

Revoke: an act of annulment, such as withdrawing an offer.

Rights and obligations: the terms of the contract set out the legal rights and obligations of the parties.

Set aside: to cancel or make void. A voidable contract is valid until it is set aside.

Simple contract: a contract that does not have to be in any particular form.

Special notice: if a claimant wants to claim damages for losses that do not arise naturally from the contract, but could reasonably be supposed by both parties to be a probable result of a breach, then he should give the other party special notice of such probable losses.

Specific performance: a court order to make a person carry out his obligations under a contract. This is a discretionary remedy and will not be ordered if damages are a sufficient remedy.

Suspension of performance: in the common law, there is no general principle allowing an innocent party to suspend his own performance because the other party is in breach.

Termination: a contract is terminated when it is brought to an end. The term termination should be used rather than rescission where the contract is discharged by **breach**.

Terms: the promises and stipulations that are part of a contract. Not all the terms in a contract are of equal importance. English law categorises terms as conditions or warranties.

Third party: one who is not a party to the original contract.

Undue influence: refers to improper pressure other than violence to make someone enter into a contract.

Unfair contract terms: refers in particular to the use of exclusion clauses.

Vitiating factor: a defect that was present in the agreement at the time the contract was made. The defect is sufficiently serious to have the contract set aside. Vitiating factors include misrepresentation, mistake, duress and undue influence.

Void: a void contract is one that was never legally valid and is without legal effect.

Voidable: a voidable contract is a valid contract, but it contains a vitiating factor. That means it can be made void if one of the parties takes steps to rescind the contract.

Warranty: is a term of lesser importance than a condition. Its breach would not give the innocent party the option to end the contract, but it would give the innocent party the right to claim damages. In the USA, the term warranty is used in particular in the context of the sale of goods. The goods must conform to the representations made by the seller. If they do not, the buyer can bring an action for breach of warranty.

CONTRACT LAW CASE DISCUSSION

Mr Jones is a second-hand car dealer. Miss Smith wants a second-hand car, but tells Mr Jones that she is only interested in buying a car which has done less than 10,000 miles. He offers Miss Smith a 1998 Ford Escort for a reasonable price. During the trial run, Miss Smith tells him she likes the car, the price is acceptable, but she repeats that she only wants the car if it has done less than 10,000 miles. Mr Jones says: 'Of course it has not done more than 10,000 miles. Look at the milometer!' The milometer shows 7,000 miles.

However, what Mr Jones said was not true. The milometer has been tampered with and Miss Smith finds out that the car has done at least 30,000 miles.

Advise Miss Smith as to her legal position.

CONTRACT LAW KNOWLEDGE QUESTIONS

1. For the formation of a contract, **consideration** is one of the three basic requirements to make an agreement into a contract. What are the other two requirements?

2. What is the doctrine of **privity of contract**?

3. What is the difference between an **express term** and an **implied term**?

4. In English law, **contractual terms** are classified according to their importance; a term may be of fundamental importance or it may be only a minor term. Name these two categories of terms.

5. What is the purpose of an **exclusion clause** in a contract?

6. Explain the term **rescission**.

7. What is a **misrepresentation**?

8. What is the difference between **discharge by frustration** and **discharge by breach**?

9. Explain what is meant by **remoteness of damage**.

10. What is **specific performance**?

5 Company law terminology

COMPANY LAW TERMINOLOGY IN CONTEXT

The larger law firms and commercial enterprises tend to be internationally orientated. If you have spent any time in the company law department of a large law firm, or company, you will know that most of the paperwork is in English. A familiarity with the terminology of company law is therefore a must.

Two points should be borne in mind:

- Even though the company law of EU Member States has gone through a process of harmonisation, there are still some differences between the Member States. This affects the use of terminology.
- There are also differences in terminology between England and the USA, which students and practitioners should be aware of to avoid confusion. A good example is the word **company** itself, which is used rather differently by English lawyers than by American lawyers.

This chapter will first take a brief look at the terminology associated with unincorporated forms of business organisation. It will then focus on the terminology of company law.

5.1   Which form of business enterprise?

If you are going to set up a business, you must choose whether to operate as a sole trader, a partnership or a company. To make an informed choice, you must be aware of the legal structure of these different types of business organisation.

One of the main legal distinctions in the classification of business enterprises is between enterprises that are **incorporated** and those that are **unincorporated**. The distinction is a very important one because of its legal consequences. Incorporation makes a business a separate **legal person**. An unincorporated business organisation is not a separate legal person. It is a **natural person** because the person (or persons) and the business are seen as one and the same.

5.2   Unincorporated business organisations

5.2.1   Sole trader

A **sole trader** is basically a one-man business. If a person operates a business alone, the business and the owner are one. The sole trader is entitled to the profits of the business but he is also responsible for its losses. If the business is in debt, then the sole trader is **personally liable** for those debts. This means that his private property, for example his home, can be called upon in order to pay off the creditors.

The advantage of operating as a sole trader is that you are your own boss. The disadvantage is that if your business fails, you risk losing everything.

> N | Note: a sole trader is called a **sole proprietorship** in the USA.

5.2.2   Partnership

If you would rather work together with other people than alone, you might like to set up a partnership. A **partnership** is just a term used to describe the relationship between people who carry on a business together, with the intention of making a profit from that business. Partnerships are also referred to in English law as **firms** and the name under which their business is carried on is called the firm name.

There are a number of differences between the legal structure of a partnership and that of a company.

Table 1. *The characteristics of a partnership*

Legal person	Legal requirements	Decisions	Tax	Liability
No. Natural person.	Few.	A partner can bind other partners as an agent of the firm.	Income tax.	Personal liability of the partners Joint and several liability.

- **Unincorporated**, it is not a separate person in law. It is formed by the individual partners who are **natural persons**.
- There are few legal requirements as to how a partnership should be set up. You do not need to **register** a partnership. You do not even need a written agreement between the people who are going to form the partnership. However, it is usual, and indeed sensible, to make a written agreement, which is called a **deed** or **articles of partnership**.
- In English law, every partner is an **agent** of the firm. That means if a partner enters into a contract that is to do with the business of the partnership, it is as if the whole firm entered the contract. But a partner can only bind the firm if the contract is in the **ordinary course of the business**. For example, if a partner in a software firm enters into a contract to buy himself a private yacht, that would not be anything to do with the business of the partnership and then the other partners are not bound by the contract.
- The partners pay income tax as they are taxed as natural persons.
- If the partnership goes into debt, and the partnership is **dissolved**, the creditors will be paid out of the **partnership property**. However, if that is not enough, the partners are then **personally liable**. That means their personal property can be taken to pay off the debts. **Joint and several liability** applies: a creditor can sue all the partners or any single one of them for the money he is owed.

The advantage of a partnership is that there are fewer legal requirements for a partnership than for a company. The disadvantage is that partners can be personally liable for the debts of the partnership. It is because of the personal liability of partners, that some partnerships are structured in a different way in order to limit that liability. These are the **limited partnership** and the **limited liability partnership**.

> _N_ Note: in English law, the word **firm** describes a partnership and it cannot be used to describe a **company**. A firm cannot be a company. That is different in the USA. American lawyers often use the two words interchangeably. This is because, under American law, the term company also covers the term partnership. Take the following example from an American textbook on corporate governance: 'Furthermore, when one firm controls a number of other firms held in the form of subsidiaries, the parent firm is referred to as a holding company.' Such a sentence would not be possible in an English legal textbook.

5.3   Incorporated business organisations

The most important form of incorporated business organisation is the **registered company**. In English law, a company is defined as an association of persons formed for the purpose of carrying on business in the name of that association. It must be **registered** and is then legally **incorporated**.

If you set up a registered company, the company is a separate **legal person**, separate from you. The advantage of the company being a legal person is that, in general, you will not be personally liable for the wrongful acts or the debts of the company. The disadvantage of choosing to do business in the form of a company is that there are many legal requirements which you must fulfil.

Table 2. The characteristics of a company

Legal person	Legal requirements	Decisions	Tax	Liability
Yes. It is incorporated as a separate person at law.	Many. A company must register and make public its annual accounts.	The main decision is the board making body of directors. Shareholders in the AGM can veto or approve board resolutions.	Corporation tax.	In general no personal liability. Directors will only be held personally liable for a breach of duty. Shareholders have no personal liability for the debts of the company once they have paid for their shares.

N Note 1: the American legal term for such a registered company is **corporation**. English terminology also refers to corporations; it means either a company or a public authority that has been incorporated. The English often use the term corporation to indicate a large company, for example Shell or Unilever.

N Note 2: in this chapter, references to the term 'company' will be used in the English legal sense of the word to mean only an incorporated, separate legal person.

5.4 The legal structure of a registered company

The most popular form of registered company is the **limited liability company** (which is the one used as a standard company in this chapter). If a company is a limited liability company, **shareholders** are not personally liable for the debts of the company. Once they have paid for their shares, their liability ends.

> N | Note: shareholders may also be referred to as **members** or **owners** of the company.

Legal person
A company's incorporation creates three separate pillars:
- the company;
- its membership; and
- its management.

Once registered, a company becomes a separate person in law. As a legal person, it can, for example, own property, commit crimes and torts and enter into contracts.

While each individual company is a separate legal person, it is common to find groups of companies headed by a **holding company** (or **parent company**). The business of a holding company consists wholly or mainly in holding shares or securities in one or more companies in the group, which are its **subsidiaries**. A holding company must produce **group accounts**.

5.5 Formation of a company

The creation of a new company needs a **promoter**. The promoter's task is to set up a registered company. The promoter will deal with administrative aspects, such as registering the company, but he may also be active in acquiring **capital** for the company and entering into preliminary agreements.

This may require the promoter to enter into **pre-incorporation contracts**. A pre-incorporation contract is where a person enters into a contract on behalf of a company that has not yet been incorporated.

> N | Note: a promoter can be a person, an agency or another company.

5.5.1 Registration

To become incorporated, the company must **register**. Once registered, the company will be issued a **certificate of incorporation**. Incorporation in both England and the Netherlands requires detailed documentation that outlines the structure of the company. The procedure can easily take weeks.

> **N** Note 1: in the USA, reference is made to **filing** rather than registering.

> **N** Note 2: in general, incorporation is a simpler matter in the USA. The requirements of the states vary, but the state of Delaware is famous for its speed in incorporating businesses, with documentation that is sometimes no longer than a page.

5.5.2 Types of companies

In English law, an important distinction is made between a **public company** and a **private company**. This distinction is found in many civil law countries, for example Germany and the Netherlands.

Public company
A **public company** may offer its shares to, and borrow money from, the public. For example, as Manchester United football club is now also a public company, you could buy shares in it and become a shareholder. To be incorporated, a public company must have a minimum subscribed **share capital**.
It must be clear whether the company is a public or a private company. For example, the name of an English public company must end with the suffix **public limited company**, which is abbreviated to 'Plc' and a Dutch public company would end with NV.

Private company
A **private company**, unlike a public company, may not offer its shares to, or borrow money from, the public at large. In England a private company does not need a minimum level of share capital to register or commence trading. This is not necessarily the

case in other EU countries. In the Netherlands, for example, a private company is also required to have a minimum level of share capital before incorporation, although that amount is less than the amount required for a public company.

The name of an English private company must end with the word **limited**, abbreviated to 'Ltd'. In the Netherlands, you can see that a company is a private company because it has the initials BV after the name.

5.6   The company's constitution

When you register a company, you must hand in the documents that deal with the company's constitution. The constitution of English companies is governed by two main documents: the **memorandum** and the **articles of association**. In practice the memorandum and articles of association are often attached together. In the Netherlands, for example, there is one main constitutional document (the 'statuten'): it contains the same information as the two English documents.

> *N* Note: the Dutch term 'statuten' is usually translated by the English term articles of association.

Memorandum of association
The **memorandum of association** is primarily concerned with the external regulation of the company. It contains a number of compulsory clauses:
*   the name of the company, whether it is a limited liability company and whether it is a private or public limited company;
*   the address of the registered office;
*   the **objects clause**: this clause states the business or the purpose for which the company was incorporated;
*   the nominal capital of the company and its arrangement of shares.

Articles of association
The **articles of association** deal primarily with the internal running of the company. The document includes articles on:

- organising general meetings;
- the appointment and powers of directors; and
- the types of shares that can be issued.

The articles of association are the bible of the company. If you are a director and act in a way that conflicts with the articles, you will be in breach of your director's duty. Articles are **binding** but they may, nevertheless, be altered by **special resolution** (this is where a 75% majority of the shareholders vote in favour of the change).

> N | Note: in the USA, generally only one document needs to be filed: this document is often referred to as the **articles of incorporation**. It is not as detailed as the English or Dutch documentation. The rules for the internal running of the corporation are set out in a separate document, the **bylaws**, which does not have to be filed.

5.7   Financing the company

There are two main ways of bringing **capital** into the company: by issuing shares or by borrowing money.

5.7.1   Shares

Shares represent the investment of a shareholder in a company. **Share capital** is the term given to the capital raised by issuing the company's shares. Can a company issue as many shares as it wants when it wants to? The answer to that is no: the amount is fixed in the company's memorandum. It is called the **authorised share capital**: the total **nominal value** of the shares that a company is authorised to issue.

> N | Note: in the USA, it is common to refer to shareholders as **stockholders**.

Offering shares to the public
If a public company invites the public to buy its shares, it must give accurate information about those shares. This information is contained in:

- a **prospectus** when shares are being issued by a new company and
- in **listing particulars** if the company is not new, but already listed on the Stock Exchange.

It is against the law to put any untrue information in these documents. It is also against the law for a private company to offer its shares to the public.

Information concerning the shares may affect the market value. For this reason, in English law it is a criminal offence for a person to use confidential information about the company in order to buy or sell the shares at a profit. This practice is known as **insider dealing** or **insider trading**.

5.7.2 Loan capital

Share capital is not the only source of finance for a company. Credit arrangements are also vital. The term **loan capital** refers to money borrowed by a company, in its capacity as a legal person. A **bond** is a certificate issued by a public company, promising to repay the borrowed money at a specified time, at a fixed rate of interest. A document that acknowledges a credit arrangement between a company and a **creditor** is also known as a **debenture**. A person who has a debenture is also referred to as a **debenture holder**.

The person or institution lending the money may be either a secured creditor, meaning the lender has some form of security in case the company later fails to pay back the loan, or an unsecured creditor, in which case the loan is not protected.

5.8   The management of the company

The term **corporate governance** is often used to describe the way in which companies are run. A company is a separate legal person but people must manage it. The directors form the management of the company.

5.8.1 Director

In English law, there is no legal definition of **director**. It can be 'any person occupying the position of director, by whatever name called'. This means that a person need not formally have the title 'director' to be one. In practice, the term is applied to anyone who is responsible for the management of a company, because he is on the board of directors and takes part in the decision-making. A director of a company need not be a natural person; a company could act as a director of another company. A director is said to be an **officer** of a company.

Appointment of directors
All directors, except the very first directors, are appointed according to the rules laid down in the articles of association. The articles usually state that directors will be appointed on an **ordinary resolution** (in other words, if a majority of the shareholders vote for them).

Types of directors
There are various types of director:

- **Executive director** (USA: often referred to as an **inside director**): this is usually a full-time officer of a company, with the task of day-to-day management. Many company directors hold service contracts, in other words, they are salaried employees of the company. Sometimes, in small private companies, each shareholder is an executive director. In that case, it is possible that they are not paid as directors.
- **Non-executive director** (USA: often referred to as an **outside**, **independent** or **non-management director**): a non-executive director is not a salaried employee, nor is he responsible for the day-to-day management of the company. Non-executive directors are usually chosen for their expertise or public recognition in some particular field. They are not salaried employees, but they are paid for their services. The idea is that they are independent of the company and can be objective.
- **Managing director** (or **chief executive officer**, the **CEO**): this is the director who is in charge of the whole company.

5.8.2   Board of directors

The **board of directors** consists of all the individually appointed directors. At its head is the **chairman**, who may or may not also be the managing director.

The board has general management powers, as laid down in the company's articles of association. It is the major decision-making body of the company. It can also delegate powers to committees of one or more directors, or to a managing director or other executive directors. The board has to answer to the shareholders.

> ^N Note: in some countries, for example the Netherlands and Germany, there may be two boards: a board of directors and a **supervisory board**. The task of the supervisory board is to advise and supervise the board of directors. Small companies may elect to have a supervisory board, but large companies must have a supervisory board as well as a board of directors.
> Be aware that the English and Americans do not have supervisory boards and often tend to find the whole idea a rather odd one.

5.8.3   Directors' duties

Although the directors run a company, they cannot treat it as if it were their own property. So if you are a director, you owe duties to the company. You hold your duties to the company as a whole, in other words you are responsible to the shareholders as a body and not to individual shareholders. **Directors' duties** are of two main types: a duty of care and skill, and fiduciary duties.

The duty of care and skill
This **duty of care and skill** is comparable to the American **business judgment rule**. It is basically a duty not to act **negligently** (see Chapter 3) in managing the company. You are not liable if you have done your best, but you have made a mistake because you did not have specialist knowledge or experience. For example, if you are a director of a life insurance company, that does not mean you have the knowledge of a doctor. The most important thing is that you have acted honestly for the benefit of the company.

Fiduciary duties

Take the following case: company X wants to **take over** company Y. A director is appointed to make a report on the advantages and disadvantages of this possible take over. That director, however, will make £500,000 if the take over goes ahead. By agreeing to write the report, he has put himself in an impossible position: his personal interests could prevent him from giving independent and impartial advice to company X. If he recommends a take over he gets £500,000; if he does not, he gets nothing. His duty to the company and his personal interests are hopelessly at odds.

The rules concerning **fiduciary duties** are strict. As a director, you must always act with honesty and integrity. You must use your powers for the benefit of the company and not for your own benefit. Where there is a **conflict of interest** between a director's personal interests and those of the company, those of the company must come first. That means, in our example, if you honestly believe the take over is not in the interests of the company, that is what your report must say, even if you will lose the £500,000.

A director should, however, take care not to put himself in such a conflict of interest situation. As a director you are under a duty to **disclose** to the company any personal interests, which could cause a conflict of interest situation. If you act against the interests of the company and in your own interest, you will be in **breach of directors' duties**. A director could be **personally liable** for such a breach.

5.9   Auditor

All company **annual accounts** have to be checked by an auditor unless the company is a 'small company', having a turnover of less than a certain amount. An **auditor** is an accountant whose duty it is to investigate and report upon the company's accounts. Although paid by the company, an auditor must remain independent.

5.10   Disputes between shareholders and management

The board of directors can put forward its decisions, in the form of **resolutions**, to be voted on by the shareholders at the **annual general meeting** (AGM).
In effect it is the **majority shareholders** who make the company decisions. It is difficult for **minority shareholders** to stop a resolution being passed if the majority of the shareholders are in favour of it. In general, minority shareholders cannot look to the courts for support if they are dissatisfied, as the courts will not interfere in matters of internal management.
But what if the management is guilty of fraud, or the directors are in breach of their fiduciary duties, or your rights as a shareholder have been ignored? In certain circumstances, individual members can go to court. This is called bringing a **minority action**. Shareholders can defeat the board of directors by taking action on behalf of the company to prevent wrongdoing or to enforce their own personal rights. An action by a minority shareholder (or minority shareholders) is either a **derivative action**, if the shareholder is suing because of a wrong to the company, or a personal action, if brought by a member to enforce a personal right.

5.11   The company in default

It may be the case that a company has failed to repay a loan, or the interest on a loan, to a creditor. This is an **event of default**. The creditor can then appoint a **receiver** to go into the company and make it comply with the terms of the loan. Receivers are often solicitors or accountants.

> ^N Note: in English legal terminology there is a distinction between a **receiver** and a **liquidator**. A receiver and a liquidator have separate functions, although physically they may be the same person. A receiver is appointed to help a creditor obtain payment of a debt. He is not there to bring a company to an end: this is the task of a liquidator.

5.12 Winding up a registered company

If a company is **insolvent** (another term for **bankruptcy**), it will have to stop trading and be brought to an end. A winding up **petition** is then handed in to the court. The company is kept 'alive' as a legal person just as long as is necessary to sort out all of it affairs. This process is known as **winding up**. Once the process of winding up is complete, the **liquidation** of a company has been achieved.

The role of the liquidator

A **liquidator** is appointed to wind up the company. Once appointed, only the liquidator may deal with the **assets** of the company. His role is to take control of the company, gather in the assets belonging to the company and pay off the creditors.

There is a fixed **order of priority** in a liquidation. The liquidator cannot choose whom he will pay out and in what order. He must work according to a fixed list. Each category of creditors on the list is paid off in full before moving on to the next category on the list. That means, if there are few assets, creditors lower down on the list will get little or nothing. As you can imagine, creditors with security are in a better position than creditors without security.

Alternatives to winding up

There are circumstances in which winding up the company would not be the best option for the creditors. The company could attempt to reach an understanding with the creditors to avoid insolvency procedures. In some cases, the best option for all concerned may be not to wind up the company, but to help the company get up and running again.

- **Voluntary arrangement**: here a legally binding, voluntary arrangement is made between the company and its creditors. It could be that an agreement is made with the creditors to settle a debt immediately by repaying only part of it or a plan is drawn up to offer a way of paying debts and avoiding insolvency.
- **Administration order**: it may be there is still hope that the company can survive if it is given a chance. In that case, an **administration order** puts the company management into

the hands of a special **administrator**. The administrator then runs the business. The administrator must be given the opportunity to get the company running in that time. That is why no creditors can demand payment while the order is in place. The order creates a so-called **moratorium**, or **suspension of payments**, for a fixed period.

COMPANY LAW VOCABULARY

Administrator: a practitioner appointed by an **administration order**. His task is to save the company from being wound up by getting it up and running again.

Agent: a person given the authority by a principal to enter into contracts on the principal's behalf.

Annual accounts: a detailed record of a company's financial situation that must be produced each year.

Annual general meeting (AGM): meeting of the shareholders of a company, which takes place once a year.

Articles of association: document which regulates the way a company's internal affairs are managed. It consists of regulations governing the rights of the members and the internal structure of the company.

Articles of incorporation: document filed in the USA to incorporate a company.

Articles or deed of partnership: written agreement setting out the structure of a partnership. It is not a legal requirement.

Assets: property owned by a person or company that has monetary value.

Auditor: a member of a recognised body of accountants who examines (called auditing) a company's annual accounts.

Authorised share capital: this is the amount of capital a company can raise by selling its shares.

Bankruptcy: technically, in English law, this term applies where an individual is unable to pay his debts. A company is said to be insolvent, an individual bankrupt. Informally, it is used to describe both. In the USA, the distinction is not made.

Binding: legally enforceable.

Board of directors: the board consists of the individual directors. It is the ultimate decision-making body of a company and determines the delegation of power.

Bond: a certificate issued by a public company (or government) promising to repay borrowed money at a specified time and at a fixed rate of interest.

Breach of director's duties: where a director has acted in a way inconsistent with the duty of care and skill and fiduciary duties owed to the company.

Bylaws: in the USA, the internal structural aspects of the corporation are set out in bylaws, which do not have to be filed.

Capital: the net worth of a company; money, property and any other assets.

Certificate of incorporation: this is issued to a registered company on incorporation.

Chairman: an appointed director who presides over meetings of the board of directors and general meetings.

Company: in English law, an association of persons formed for the purposes of a business carried on in the name of the association. It is legally incorporated and is a legal person, separate from its individual members. In the USA, the word applies to a wide range of activities and can be used to describe private corporations as well as partnerships.

Company constitution: in English law, the constitution of a company is governed by two main documents, the memorandum and articles of association.

Conflict of interest: where there is a conflict of interests between a director's personal interests and those of the company, those of the company must prevail.

Corporate governance: term often used to describe the way in which companies are directed and controlled.

Corporation: in English law, a legal body, such as a limited company or public authority, which has been incorporated. It is often used to indicate a large company. Likewise, in the USA, the term also means an association of shareholders that is a separate legal person.

Creditor: one to whom a debt is owed.

Debenture: a document acknowledging a debt for a capital sum that is to be repaid by a company on a certain date, with interest payable at a fixed rate. In the London financial markets, the word debenture is used primarily to denote a secured loan. Reference may be made to a naked debenture, which is a debt without security. In the USA, a debenture is usually an unsecured loan.

Debenture holder: a creditor of the company.

Derivative action: an action by a minority shareholder (or minority shareholders) is a derivative action if the shareholder is suing in the name of the company.

Director: in English law, there is no legal definition of director but, according to legislation, the term director includes any person occupying the position of director, by whatever name called.

Directors' duties: include the duty of care and skill and fiduciary duties.

Disclosure: to disclose involves revealing details about an act or transaction. Directors are under a duty to disclose any personal interest that could lead to a conflict of interest situation.

Dissolution: here the term refers to bringing a partnership to an end.

Dividend: a sum paid to shareholders by a company when in profit, the amount being in proportion to their shareholding.

Duty of care and skill: the so-called **business judgment rule** means that a director must not be negligent in the management of his company, but that he will not be liable for mere errors of judgment.

Event of default: an event that means a creditor can now call in his loan.

Executive director (**inside director**): this is usually a full-time officer employed by the company to manage company business.

Fiduciary duties: a director is under an obligation to exercise his powers for the benefit of the company and not for his own benefit. He owes a general duty of trust, honesty and integrity towards the company.

Filing: in the USA, reference is made to filing rather than registering a company.

Firm: partnerships are referred to in English law as firms and the name under which their business is carried on is called the firm name. In the USA, the word company is used synonymously with firm, whereas in English law a firm is never a company.

Group accounts: group accounts must be drawn up by a holding company where there is a parent/subsidiary relationship.

Holding company (or **parent company**): the business of a holding company consists wholly or mainly in holding shares or securities in one or more companies within the group, which are its subsidiary companies.

Incorporation: the issue of an incorporation certificate creates an independent legal person.

Insider dealing/trading: using confidential information about a company in order to buy or sell its shares at a profit.

Insolvent: a company is insolvent if it can no longer pay its debts. **Insolvency** procedures will then be followed.

Joint and several liability: partners may be collectively liable and individually liable.

Legal person: once registered, a company becomes a separate person in law. This artificial legal person can own property, commit crimes and torts and conclude contracts.

Limited liability company: in England, a registered company where the shareholders' liability in the event of a winding up is limited to any amount that has not yet been paid for their shares. It is the most usual form of trading company. The American limited liability company is not the direct equivalent of the English limited liability company, as it is something of a hybrid between a corporation and a partnership.

Limited liability partnership: is a separate legal entity, giving its members the benefit of limited liability while keeping the internal structure of a partnership.

Limited partnership: one where a distinction is made between general partners and limited partners. Limited partners have invested in the company, but have no active function. These limited partners are not personally liable for the debts of the partnership beyond the capital they have invested already.

Liquidation: a company is brought to an end, often because of insolvency.

Liquidator: the one appointed to supervise the winding up of a company.

Listing particulars: document offering shares or debentures to the public where the company is listed already.

Loan capital: capital that has been obtained on credit.

Majority shareholder: one who holds sufficient shares in a company to influence the decision-making.

Management: those who direct or run a business.

Managing director (or **chief executive officer**): a director in charge of the management of a company.

Members: the members of a company are the **shareholders**.

Memorandum of association: legal document regulating a company's external activities. It states the company's name, objectives, registered office, domicile, the amount of the company's nominal capital and the number and amount of shares.

Minority action: an action brought by a single shareholder or small number of shareholders.

Minority shareholder: one who does not hold sufficient shares in a company to command an influential position.

Moratorium: a **suspension of payments** is initiated for a fixed period so that no-one except the administrator can deal with the assets of a company during that period.

Natural person: this is a human being rather than an artificial person, such as a registered company. A natural person has the right to participate in a wider variety of legal transactions than a legal person.

Nominal value: the face value of a share rather than its market value.

Non-executive director (outside, independent or **non-management director):** this is not a salaried employee and he is not actively involved in daily management.

Objects clause: a clause in the memorandum of association setting out the purpose for which the company was incorporated.

Officer (of a company): one invested with authority for a particular position. In English law, a director is an officer of a company.

Order of priority: the liquidator must pay creditors according to a list of priorities.

Ordinary course of business: a partnership will be bound by contracts entered into by an individual partner, if covering the usual type of business conducted by the firm.

Ordinary resolution: a simple majority vote by shareholders.

Owners: the owners of a company are the **shareholders**.

Partnership: the relationship between persons carrying on a business in common with a view to profit. It is unincorporated and therefore not a separate legal person.

Partnership property: property that is jointly owned by the partners. Assets that have not been transferred to the partnership remain the property of the individual partners.

Personal liability: where an individual is held liable, for example, a sole trader is held liable for the debts of his business.

Petition: certain civil actions are started by petition, for example, a winding up petition is presented to the court in order to liquidate a company.

Pre-incorporation contract: where a person enters into a contract on behalf of a company which has not yet been formed.

Private company: a company that may not offer its shares and debentures to the public.

Promoter: one who organises the setting up of a new company.

Prospectus: document in which shares or debentures are offered to the public for the first time.

Public company: a public company must have a minimum subscribed share capital. It may seek finance by offering its shares and debentures to the public. If it is a public limited company, it is one incorporated with limited liability.

Receiver: when the company has failed to repay a debt to a creditor, a receiver will take control of the property in question for the benefit of the creditor. He is not appointed to wind up a company.

Register: to be noted on an official list; a **registered company** is listed on the Companies Registry.

Resolution: a formal proposal, usually voted upon at a meeting.

Share capital: the total amount which a company's shareholders have contributed or are liable to contribute as payment for their shares.

Shareholder: one who holds shares in a company.

Shares: interest held by a shareholder in a company, measured by a sum of money for the purposes of liability and **dividend**.

Sole proprietorship: the American term for a sole trader.

Sole trader: an unincorporated, one-man business, where the owner of the business is personally liable for any losses arising from his business.

Special resolution: a company resolution, which is only valid if approved by 75% of the votes cast at a meeting. Twenty-one days notice must be given.

Stockholders: in the USA, shareholders are referred to as stockholders (as they own one or more shares of stock).

Subsidiary: a subsidiary company is one that is held by a parent company.

Supervisory board: in some countries, companies may have a supervisory board that advises and supervises the board of directors. The USA and England do not have a two-tier system of management, although they may use advisory committees.

Take over: where one company wants to take over the control of another company.

Unincorporated: a business organisation that is not incorporated is not a separate legal person.

Voluntary arrangement: rather than enter into winding up proceedings, a company can make a voluntary arrangement with its creditors for repayment, if supervised by a qualified insolvency practitioner.

Winding up: process by which a registered company is dissolved. A winding up can be compulsory or voluntary.

COMPANY LAW CASE DISCUSSION

Giles is a director of Acme Ltd, a car company. He also has a large shareholding in Peterson Ltd, but Acme does not know this. Peterson enters into contractual negotiations with Acme to develop a new engine. Giles encourages Acme to enter into a contract with Peterson, because if Peterson gets the contract it will double the value of his shareholding in Peterson.

Acme's articles of association state that loans above £300,000 cannot be granted unless the board of directors have agreed to the loan. Yet without consulting the board, Giles agrees to lend Peterson £500,000 of Acme's money to help pay for researching the new engine.

Acme finds out about Giles' shareholding in Peterson and the loan of £500,000. Explain to Acme what its rights are in company law.

COMPANY LAW KNOWLEDGE QUESTIONS

1. A partnership is **unincorporated**. What does that mean?

2. What is meant by the term **legal person**?

3. Why would an English lawyer never describe a company as a **firm**?

4. What may a **public company** do that a private company may not?

5. If a company is a **limited liability company**, what does that mean?

6. What is the purpose of **articles of association**?

7. Explain the difference between an **executive director** and a **non-executive director**?

8. What is a **derivative action**?

9. What are the **fiduciary duties** owed by a director to a company?

10. If the company has gone into **liquidation**, who is appointed to wind up the company and what is his task?

Bibliography

Andrews, Neil, English Civil Procedure: Fundaments of the New Civil Justice System, Oxford University Press, 2003.

Baker, C.D., Tort, Sweet & Maxwell, 1996.

Cheshire, Fifoot & Furmston's Law of Contract, Butterworths, 2001.

Civil Procedure, White Book, Sweet & Maxwell, 1999.

Colin, P.H., Dictionary of Law, Peter Collin Publishing, 2000.

Dunné, J.M. van, Verbintenissenrecht, Kluwer, 2001.

Ellison, John & Tom Harrison, Business Law, Harrison Law Publishing, 2000.

Essential Law Series (Cavendish Publishing) revision aids on: tort (Richard Owen) and company law (Nicholas Bourne).

Franken, H., Encyclopedie van de rechtswetenschap, Kluwer, 2003.

Gifis, Steven H., Law Dictionary, Barron's Legal Guides, 1996.

Glendon, Mary Ann, Michael Wallace Gordon & Christopher Osakwe, Comparative Legal Traditions: Text, Materials and Cases, West Publishing Co, 1994.

Griffin, Stephen, Company Law: Fundamental Principles, Pitman Publishing, 1994.

Harvard Business Review on Corporate Governance, Harvard Business School Press, 1999.

Jolowicz, J.A., On Civil Procedure, Cambridge, 2000.

Keenan, Denis, Smith & Keenan's Advanced Business Law, Pearson Education Limited, 2000.

Kite, Kevin L., Adam Rappaport & Craig A. Sperling, Blond's Commercial Law, S&G Publishing, 1995.

Morrison, Alan B. (ed.), Fundamentals of American Law, Oxford University Press, 1996.

Nutshell Series (Sweet & Maxwell) revision aids on: company law (Francis Rose), consumer law (Sandra Silberstein), English legal system (Penny Darbyshire) and contract law (Robert Duxbury).

Schilfgaarde, P. van, Van de BV en de NV, Gouda Quint, 1998.

Walker, Ronald & Richard Ward, Walker & Walker's English Legal System, Butterworths, 1998.

Weir, Tony, Tort Law, Clarendon Law Series, Oxford University Press, 2002.